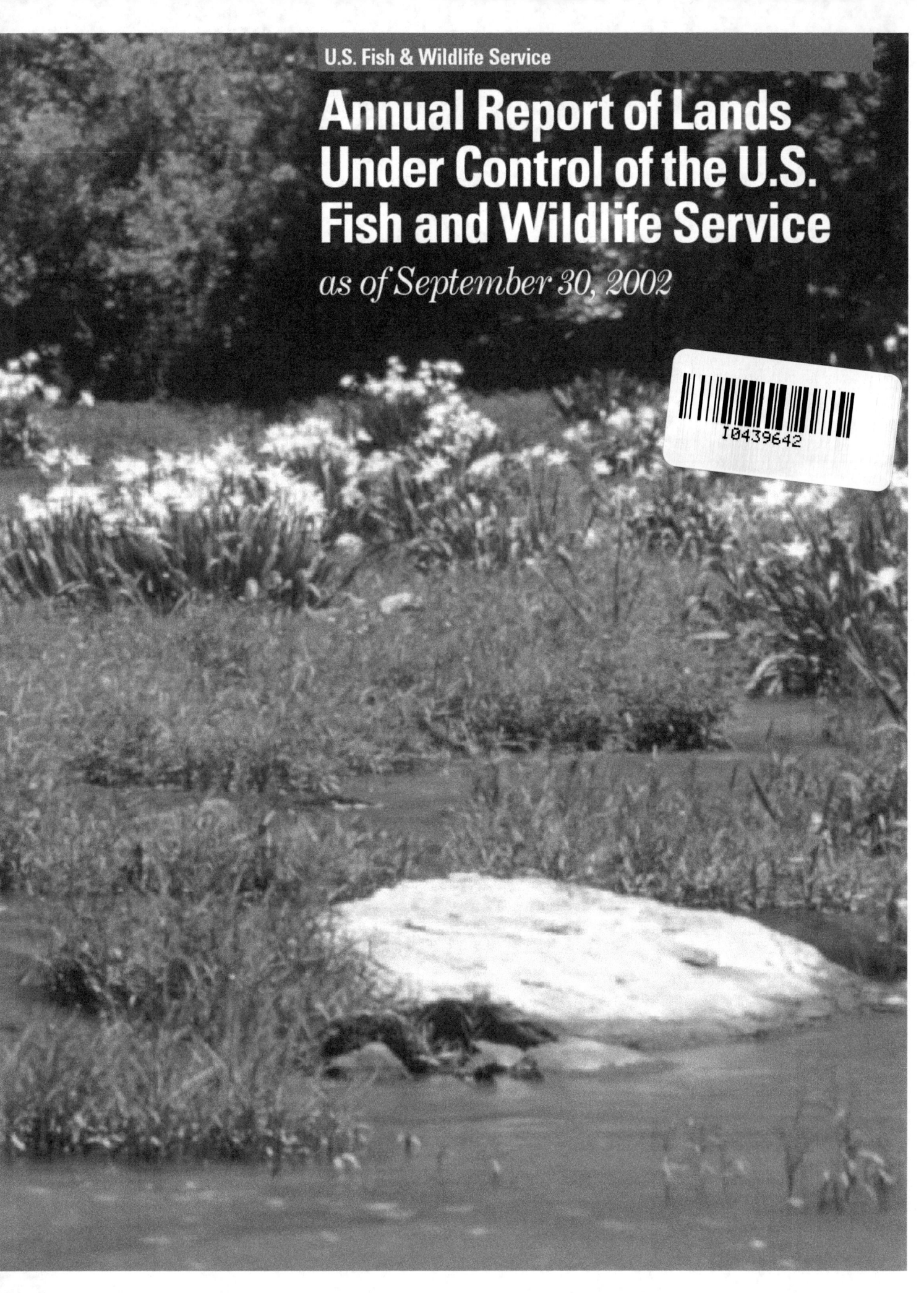

U.S. Fish & Wildlife Service

Annual Report of Lands Under Control of the U.S. Fish and Wildlife Service

as of September 30, 2002

On the cover:
Cahaba River
National Wildlife Refuge

On October 19, 2000, H.R. 4286, the Cahaba River National Wildlife Refuge Establishment Act, was signed into Public Law 106-331. This law established the Cahaba River National Wildlife Refuge in Bibb County, Alabama, and directed the Secretary of the Interior to acquire up to 3,500 acres of lands and waters within the boundary of the refuge. In partnership with The Nature Conservancy, the Service began acquiring land for the refuge in September 2002 and currently has 1,120 acres.

The Cahaba River is Alabama's longest free-flowing stream and one of the longest in the nation. This river provides diverse habitat for fish and other aquatic life due to a wide variety of geological substrates including sandstone, limestone, shale, dolomite, and chalk. The newly established Cahaba River National Wildlife Refuge lies between the confluence of the Cahaba River and Little Cahaba River and the Piper Bridge. This section of the river is extremely rich in species biodiversity, contains an extensive series of shoals vegetated with the Cahaba lilly and waterwillow, and both sides of the river are forested with loblolly, longleaf pine, and upland hardwoods. The rolling uplands around the river are typically covered with pine or mixed pine-hardwood forests.

The Cahaba River is recognized nationally for its unique biological diversity which includes rare and imperiled fish, mollusks, and plant species. Federally listed species within the new refuge include two fishes (the Cahaba shiner and the goldline darter) and five mollusks (the upland combshell, fine-lined pocketbook, triangular kidneyshell, round rocksnail, and cylindrical lioplax). This area is also historic and potential recovery habitat for five additional mollusk species, one candidate plant species (*Aster georgianus*), and one plant species of concern (*Hymenocallis coronaria*).

Although the freshwater fauna of the Cahaba River has experienced a dramatic decline in the past 50 years, the Cahaba River is still one of the nation's most biologically diverse rivers. It is also one of the most threatened. The river currently supports 64 rare and imperiled species; 15 fish, snail, and mussel species that are federally listed; 131 species of fish, more than any other river its size in North America; and 13 species (11 aquatic snails and 2 fish) found nowhere else in the world but the Cahaba River.

Degradation of water quality in the Cahaba River has and continues to be the greatest threat to aquatic species in the river. Urbanization, sewage pollution, siltation, and strip-mining activities in the upper Cahaba River Basin are the principle causes for the decrease in water quality. Inadequately treated effluent have caused problems such as euthrophication, increased acidity and conductivity, and other changes in water chemistry. Other threats include nonpoint source pollution which originates from land surface activities and stormwater runoff.

The Cahaba River National Wildlife Refuge offers protection to a unique section of the river and, through proper management, will contribute to the recovery plan goals for several federally listed species. The primary refuge objectives are to (1) preserve and manage a unique section of the biologically significant Cahaba River, (2) protect the habitat integrity and water quality of the Cahaba River, and (3) develop and implement environmental education and interpretation programs focusing on ecosystem management and stewardship responsibilities. For several years, The Nature Conservancy has been developing partnerships with corporations, local communities, and other conservation groups to protect the Cahaba River and its unique natural resources. The Service is working with these partnerships to encourage a stream management strategy that places a high priority on conservation and restoration.

The Cahaba River NWR is located approximately 25 miles southwest of Birmingham, 25 miles southeast of Tuscaloosa, and 70 miles northwest of Montgomery. This area has outstanding potential for fish and wildlife oriented public uses such as fishing, bird watching, and environmental education. Because of its proximity to Birmingham and Tuscaloosa, school groups and visitors will have access to the refuge.

Annual Report of Lands Under Control of the U.S. Fish and Wildlife Service as of September 30, 2002

Compiled By: Division of Realty

Message from the Director

On March 14, 2003, the National Wildlife Refuge System will celebrate 100 years of extraordinary growth and achievement. A century has passed since President Theodore Roosevelt established the first national wildlife refuge at Pelican Island, Florida, sparking the American wildlife conservation movement. For those of us who work for the U.S. Fish and Wildlife Service, there could hardly be a more significant, exciting or gratifying anniversary.

The National Wildlife Refuge System has been called America's best-kept secret. During this Centennial year, we will spread the word for the System to become recognized for what it truly is, one of America's greatest national treasures, and a resounding success story for wildlife conservation.

On March 14, 1903, without fanfare, President Roosevelt signed an executive order establishing Pelican Island as a federal bird reservation, the precursor to the National Wildlife Refuge System. Subsequently, Paul Kroegel was hired to become the first national wildlife refuge manager. He was paid $1 a month. With a badge, a gun and a boat, Kroegel stood watch over Pelican Island until the 1920s. President Roosevelt would go on to establish an additional 54 national wildlife refuges during his two terms as President.

Tiny, mangrove-covered Pelican Island was the birthplace of an idea unique in the world—that wildlife and wild places should be protected. It was a proclamation on behalf of a nation with an emerging consciousness about the value of things wild and free. And it was a promise—radical for its time—to preserve wildlife and habitat for its own sake and the benefit of the American people. From this humble start at Pelican Island, the National Wildlife Refuge System has emerged.

Today, the system has grown to nearly 95 million acres. It now includes 540 refuges and more than 3,000 waterfowl production areas spread across the 50 states and several U.S. territories.

Nearly 40 million people visit our national wildlife refuges every year. These include hunters, anglers, nature lovers, birders, hikers, and photographers—they all come for many reasons and often become vocal advocates, first in line to defend and protect our refuges and the goal of wildlife conservation.

The Refuge System story is as simple and compelling as one man and one boat protecting birds on Pelican Island. One President creating one system of refuges. But the Refuge System story is also as complex and challenging as seeking to understand the intricacies of ecosystems on millions of acres of land that include tundras, deserts, forests, great rivers, marshes, mountains, prairies, estuaries and coral reefs.

During this Centennial Celebration, I'd like to encourage all Americans to get out and experience nature. There is a national wildlife refuge located within an hours drive of every major U.S. city and I'd like to see more Americans take that drive and re-connect with nature.

Refuges are living, breathing places where the ancient rhythms of life can still be heard, where nature's colors are most vibrant, and where time is measured in seasons. They are gifts to ourselves and to generations unborn—simple gifts unwrapped each time a hunter sets a decoy, an angler casts the waters, a birder lifts binoculars, or a child overturns a rock.

As we celebrate the remarkable success of the National Wildlife Refuge System during 2003, we should also heed Theodore Roosevelt's vision and warning: "Wild beasts and birds are by right not the property merely of the people who are alive today," he said, "but the property of the unknown generations, whose belongings we have no right to squander." For all of us who care about the future of wildlife in America, those words remain as much a call to action today as they were 100 years ago.

Here's to a second century of conservation on our National Wildlife Refuges.

Steve Williams

KEY TO REAL PROPERTY NUMBERS

SEPTEMBER 30, 2002

NFH National Fish Hatchery
NWR National Wildlife Refuge
WMA Wildlife Management Area

3	Neosho NFH, MO
5	Leadville NFH, CO
6	Craig Brook NFH, ME
11	Bozeman Fish Technology Cen., MT
14	Erwin NFH, TN
15	Nashua NFH, NH
17	D. C. Booth NFH, SD
18	Worm Springs NFH, GA
19	Edenton NFH, NC
22	White Sulphur Springs NFH, WV
23	Private John Allen NFH, MS
25	Pelican Island NWR, FL
26	Mammoth Spring NFH, AR
27	Breton NWR, LA
28	Stump Lake NWR, ND
29	Wichita Mountains Wildlife Ref., OK
30	Huron NWR, MI
31	Passage Key NWR, FL
32	Shell Keys NWR, LA
33	Three Arch Rocks NWR, OR
34	Copalis NWR, WA
35	Flattery Rocks NWR, WA
36	Quillayute Needles NWR, WA
38	Key NWR, FL
39	Lower Klamath NWR, CA & OR
40	Malheur NWR, OR
41	Chase Lake NWR, ND
41-1	Island Bay NWR, FL
42	Hawaiian Islands NWR, HI
44	Cold Spring NWR, OR
46	Deer Flat NWR, ID & OR
47	Minidoka NWR, ID
52	Culebra NWR, PR
53	Farallon NWR, CA
58	Fairport NFH, IA
58-1	National Bison Range, MT
59	Pittsford NFH, VT
60	Quilcene NFH, WA
61	Clear Lake NWR, CA
63	Fort Niobrara NWR, NE
65	Green Bay NWR, WI
67	Orangeburg NFH, SC
69	Gravel Island NWR, WI
73	Anaho Island NWR, NV
74	National Elk Refuge, WY
75	Saratoga NFH, WY
77	Dungeness NWR, WA
78	Mille Lacs NWR, MN
79	Big Lake NWR, AR
81	North Platte NWR, NE
82	Berkshire Trout Hatchery, MA
85	Nine-Pipe NWR, MT
86	Pablo NWR, MT
88	Sullys Hill Nat. Game Preserve, ND
91	Blackbeard Island NWR, GA
93	Upper Mississippi River Wildlife & Fish. Refuge, IL, IA, MN, WI
95	Johnston Island NWR, (Pacific Area inset)
98	Savannah NWR, GA & SC
100	McKay Creek NWR, OR
103	Upper Klamath NWR, OR
105	Pathfinder NWR, WY
108	Tishomingo NFH, OK
109	Tule Lake NWR, CA
113	Bear River Migratory Bird Ref., UT
114	Cedar Keys NWR, FL
115	Benton Lake NWR, MT
117	Salt Plains NWR, OK
118	Cape Romain NWR, SC
119	Wolf Island NWR, GA
121	Salton Sea NWR, CA
122	Sheldon NWR, NV & OR
124	St. Marks NWR, FL
125	Crescent Lake NWR, NE
126	Genoa NFH, WI
127	Natchitoches NFH, LA
128	Fallon NWR, NV
129	Hagerman NFH, ID
131	Ennis NFH, MT
133	Dexter NFH, NM
135	Lamar NFH, PA
140	Hutton Lake NWR, WY
141	Bamforth NWR, WY
142	Long Lake NWR, ND
146	Swanquarter NWR, NC
148	Blackwater NWR, MD
159	Harrison Lake NFH, VA
160	Mattamuskeet NWR, NC
162	Trempealeau NWR, WI
164	Des Lacs NWR, ND
165	J. Clark Salyer NWR, ND
167	Arrowwood NWR, ND
168	Sand Lake NWR, SD
169	Lacreek NWR, SD
170	Lostwood NWR, ND
172	Medicine Lake NWR, MT
173	Lake Andes NWR, SD
174	Squaw Creek NWR, MO
175	Choutauqua NWR, IL
176	Waubay NWR, SD
177	Red Rock Lakes NWR, MT
178	Oregon Islands NWR, OR
179	Lake Isom NWR, TN
180	Seney NWR, MI
183	Valentine NWR, NE
184	Uvalde NFH, TX
185	Upper Souris NWR, ND
187	White River NWR, AR
188	Hart Mtn. Nat. Antelope Refuge, OR
191	Muleshoe NWR, TX
192	Rice Lake NWR, MN
193	Delta NWR, LA
194	Tamarac NWR, MN
195	Bowdoin NWR, MT
196	Kellys Slough NWR, ND
199	Bitter Lake NWR, NM
200	Desert NWR, NV
201	Swan Lake NWR, MO
202	Storm Lake NWR, ND
203	Tewaukon NWR, ND
206	Ardoch NWR, ND
207	Turnbull NWR, WA
210	Willapa NWR, WA
211	Camas NWR, ID
213	Okefenokee NWR, FL & GA
214	Yazoo NWR, MS
215	Charles M. Russell NWR, MT
217	Patuxent Research Refuge, MD
218	Bosque del Apache NWR, NM
220	Moosehorn NWR, ME
221	Sacramento NWR, CA
223	Union Slough NWR, IA
224	Bombay Hook NWR, DE
225	Agassiz NWR, MN
231	Pea Island NWR, NC
232	Red Butte NWR, SD
233	Carson NFH, WA
234	Montezuma NWR, NY
238	Lake Thibodeau NWR, MT
240	Lacassine NWR, LA
241	Ruby Lake NWR, NV
242	Aransas NWR, TX
245	Sabine NWR, LA
246-1	McKinney Lake NFH, NC
247	Black Coulee NWR, MT
248	Back Bay NWR, VA
249	Hewitt Lake NWR, MT
252	Inks Dam NFH, TX
253	Hagerman NWR, TX
254	Corning NFH, AR
255	Tybee NWR, SC
257	Leavenworth NFH, WA
259	Wheeler NWR, AL
260	Valley City NFH, ND
262	West Sister Island NWR, OH
263	Cape Meares NWR, OR
267	Great White Heron NWR, FL
268	Welaka NFH, FL
269	Piedmont NWR, GA
270	Cabeza Prieta NWR, AZ
271	Kofa NWR, AZ
272	Meridian NFH, MS
274	Necedah NWR, WI
275	Carolina Sandhills NWR, SC
276	New London NFH, MN
278	Williams Creek NFH, AZ
281	Little Pend Oreille NWR, WA
286	Buffalo Lake NWR, ND
288	Canfield Lake NWR, ND
292	Florence Lake NWR, ND
295	Johnson Lake NWR, ND
306	Lake George NWR, ND
307	Lake Ilo NWR, ND
308	Lake Nettie NWR, ND
310	Lake Zahl NWR, ND
314	McLean NWR, ND
318	Shell Lake NWR, ND
320	Hobart Lake NWR, ND
322	Susquehanna NWR, MD
323	Edwin B. Forsythe NWR, NJ
324	Stewart Lake NWR, ND
325	Lake Alice NWR, ND
328	Noxubee NWR, MS
330	Little White Salmon NFH, WA
334	Entiat NFH, WA
335	Winthrop NFH, WA
340	Havasu NWR, AZ & CA
341	San Andres NWR, NM
342	Horicon NWR, WI
349	White Lake NWR, ND
350	Willow Lake NWR, ND
352	Imperial NWR, AZ & CA
356	Lake Mason NWR, MT
359	Reelfoot NWR, KY & TN
361	Creedman Coulee NWR, MT
363	Chassahowitzka NWR, FL
364	Parker River NWR, MA
365	Santee NWR, SC
369	Halfbreed Lake NWR, MT
370	Lamesteer NWR, MT
380-1	Coleman NFH, CA
381	Hailstone NWR, MT
382	Missisquoi NWR, VT
383	Chincoteague NWR, MD & VA
386	Santa Ana NWR, TX
387	Colusa NWR, CA
388	Cherox NFH, SC
389	Great Meadows NWR, MA
390	Orangeburg County NFH, SC
391	Monomoy NWR, MA
392	Mingo NWR, MO
393	Columbia NWR, WA
394	Slade NWR, ND
395	Creston NFH, MT
396	Sutter NWR, CA
400	J.N. "Ding" Darling NWR, FL
401	Tennessee NWR, TN
403	Tishomingo NWR, OK
404	Hagerman NWR, TX
406	Laguna Atascosa NWR, TX
412	Michigan Islands NWR, MI
413	Wertheim NWR, NY
414	Mark Twain NWR, IL, IA & MO
415	Crab Orchard NWR, IL
419	Stillwater NWR, NV
423	North Attleboro NFH, MA
424	Spring Creek NFH, WA
426	Bo Ginn NFH, GA
428	Hiawatha Forest NFH, MI
429	Pendills Creek NFH, MI
430	Baldhill Dam NFH, ND
433	Pinellas NWR, FL
434	Willard NFH, WA
435	Arthur Marshall Loxahatchee NWR, FL
436	Merced NWR, CA
450	Monte Vista NWR, CO
451	Presquile NWR, VA
452	Eagle Creek NFH, OR
458	Shiawassee NWR, MI
459	National Key Deer Refuge, FL
461	Kirwin NWR, KS
467	Martin NWR, MD & VA
468	Elizabeth A. Morton NWR, NY
477	Quivira NWR, KS
482	McNary NWR, WA
483	Norfolk NFH, AR
487	Audubon NWR, ND
492	Gavins Point NFH, SD
498	Holla Bend NWR, AR
501	Abernathy Fish Technology Cen., WA
501-1	Jackson NFH, WY
505	Iroquois NWR, NY
505-2	Klamath Forest NWR, OR
507	Paint Bank NFH, VA
509	Bowden NFH, WV
513	Catahoula NWR, LA
516	Pixley NWR, CA
517	War Horse NWR, MT
518	Buffalo Lake NWR, TX
519	DeSoto NWR, IA & NE
522	Fish Springs NWR, UT
523	Erie NWR, PA
524	Fish Farming Exp. Station, AR
529	Willow Beach NFH, AZ
531	Alchesay NFH, AZ
538	Kern NWR, CA
541	Great Swamp NWR, NJ
542	Modoc NWR, CA
543	Ouray NWR, UT
547	Jordan River NFH, MI
549	San Juan Islands NWR, WA
550	Mackay Islands NWR, NC & VA
551	Wapanocca NWR, AR
555	Washita NWR, OK
566-1	Garrison Dam NFH, ND
569	Ottawa NWR, OH
571	Detroit River IWR, MI
581	Wytheville NFH, VA
589	Harris Neck NWR, GA
601	Jones Hole NFH, UT
603	Delevan NWR, CA
605	Cross Creeks NWR, TN
606	Eastern NWR, ND
608	Dale Hollow NFH, TN
612	Anahuac NWR, TX
615	John Heinz NWR at Tinicum, PA
619	Greers Ferry NFH, AR
623	Beulah Fish Technology Center, WY
626	Alamosa NWR, CO
629	Pahranagat NWR, NV
630	Prime Hook NWR, DE
632	Merritt Island NWR, FL
643	Lake Woodruff NWR, FL
651	Choctaw NWR, AL
654	Mescalero NWR, NM
655	Lee Metcalf NWR, MT
664	Toppenish NWR, WA
666	Pee Dee NWR, NC
674	Clarence Cannon NWR, MO
675	Cedar Island NWR, NC
676	Cibola NWR, AZ & CA
679	Kootenai NWR, ID
680	Eufaula NWR, AL & GA
683	Hatchie NWR, TN
684	Cedar Point NWR, OH
687	Conboy Lake NWR, WA
690	Lahontan NWR, NV
690-1	Quinault NFH, WA
691	Grays Lake NWR, ID
732	Browns Park NWR, CO
733	Kooskia NFH, ID
734	Sherburne NWR, MN
736	Seedskadee NWR, WY
745	Hotchkiss NFH, CO
746	William L. Finley NWR, OR
747	Ankeny NWR, OR
748	Baskett Slough NWR, OR
749	Ridgefield NWR, WA
751	Las Vegas NWR, NM
753	Pine Island NWR, FL
754	Matlacha Pass NWR, FL
755	Coloosahatchee NWR, FL
761	Maxwell NWR, NM
763	Flint Hills NWR, KS
766	Muscatatuck NWR, IN
768	Brazoria NWR, TX
770	Rachel Carson NWR, ME
771	San Luis NWR, CA
772	Warm Springs NFH, OR
788	Aropaho NWR, CO
789	Ul Bend NWR, MT
791	Target Rock NWR, NY
792	Wolf Creek NFH, KY
794	St. Vincent NWR, FL
795	Green Lake NFH, ME
796	Bear Lake NWR, ID
800	Buck Island NWR, VI
801	Fisherman Island NWR, VA
803	Mason Neck NWR, VA
804	San Bernard NWR, TX
805	Amagansett NWR, NY
806	Oyster Bay NWR, NY
807	Hobe Sound NWR, FL
809	Umatilla NWR, OR & WA
810	Seatuck NWR, NY
811	Wassaw NWR, GA
814	Grulla NWR, NM & TX
826	Sequoyah NWR, OK
827	Ninigret NWR, RI

KEY TO REAL PROPERTY NUMBERS

SEPTEMBER 30, 2002

NFH   National Fish Hatchery
NWR   National Wildlife Refuge
WMA   Wildlife Management Area

831	San Marcos NFH, TX
834	St. Johns NWR, FL
835	Conscience Point NWR, NY
836	Julia Butler Hansen NWR, OR & WA
838	Allegheny NFH, PA
839	Minnesota Valley NWR, MN
840	Sachuest Point NWR, RI
842	Plum Tree Island NWR, VA
843	Saddle Mountain NWR, WA
845	Lewis and Clark NWR, OR
846	Nomans Land Island NWR, MA
847	Wapack NWR, NH
848	Seal Island NWR, ME
849	Thacher Island NWR, MA
850	Attwater Prairie Chicken NWR, TX
851	Meredosia NWR, IL
852	Pond Island NWR, ME
853	Nantucket NWR, MA
855	Hanalei NWR, HI
856	Humboldt Bay NWR, CA
857	Swan River NWR, MT
858	Great Dismal Swamp NWR, NC & VA
859	Huleia NWR, HI
860	Occoquan Bay NWR, VA
861	Wallops Island NWR, VA
862	White River NFH, VT
863	Rose Atoll NWR (Pacific Area Inset)
864	Franklin Island NWR, ME
865	Block Island NWR, RI
867	Amargosa Pupfish Station, NV
868	Nansemond NWR, VA
870	San Pablo Bay NWR, CA
871	Nisqually NWR, WA
872	Sevilleta NWR, NM
876	Oxbow NWR, MA
877	Cabo Rojo NWR, PR
878	Baker Island NWR (Pacific Area Inset)
879	Howland Island NWR (Pacific Area Inset)
880	Jarvis Island NWR (Pacific Area Inset)
881	Petit Manan NWR, ME
882	Mckch NFH, WA
883	Supawna Meadows NWR, NJ
884	Egmont Key NWR, FL
889	Trustom Pond NWR, RI
890	Hopper Mountain NWR, CA
898	San Francisco Bay NWR, CA
900	Optima NWR, OK
901	Hillside NWR, MS
903	Big Stone NWR, MN
904	Moody NWR, TX
906	Seal Beach NWR, CA
907	Felsenthal NWR, AR
908	D'Arbonne NWR, LA
909	Mississippi Sandhill Crane NWR, MS
910	Karl E. Mundt NWR, NB & SD
911	Pearl Harbor NWR, HI
912	Pinckney Island NWR, SC
914	Ellicott Slough NWR, CA
915	Kakahaia NWR, HI
920	Desecheo NWR, PR
921	James Campbell NWR, HI
923	Iron River NFH, WI
924	Salinas River NWR, CA
925	Morgan Brake NWR, MS
926	Panther Swamp NWR, MS
928	Green Cay NWR, VI
929	Bear Valley NWR, OR
930	Blowing Wind Cove NWR, AL
931	Upper Ouachita NWR, LA
937	Featherstone NWR, VA
939	Fox River NWR, WI
940	Lower Suwannee NWR, FL
942	Grasslands WMA, CA
943	Moapa Valley NWR, NV
944	Crocodile Lake NWR, FL
948	Bon Secour NWR, AL
949	McFaddin NWR, TX
950	Texas Point NWR, TX
965	Antioch Dunes NWR, CA
966	Butte Sink WMA, CA
957	Lower Hatchie NWR, TN
970	Kirtland Warbler WMA, MI
971	Cross Island NWR, ME
973	Mathews Brake NWR, MS
974	Banks Lake NWR, GA
977	Overflow NWR, AR
981	Castle Rock NWR, CA
982	Tijuana Slough NWR, CA
984	Lower Rio Grande Valley NWR, TX
985	Watercress Darter NWR, AL
988	Bogue Chitto NWR, LA & MS
991	Alaska Maritime NWR, AK
992	Alaska Peninsula NWR, AK
993	Arctic NWR, AK
994	Becharof NWR, AK
995	Innoko NWR, AK
996	Izembek NWR, AK
997	Kanuti NWR, AK
998	Kenai NWR, AK
999	Kodiak NWR, AK
1000	Koyukuk NWR, AK
1001	Nowitno NWR, AK
1002	Selawik NWR, AK
1003	Tetlin NWR, AK
1004	Togiak NWR, AK
1005	Yukon Delta NWR, AK
1006	Yukon Flats NWR, AK
1008	Bears Bluff NFH, SC
1009	Fern Cave NWR, AL
1012	Richard Cronin NFH, MA
1015	San Bernardino NWR, AZ
1016	Blue Ridge NWR, CA
1018	Tensas River NWR, LA
1019	Protection Island NWR, WA
1021	Bandon Marsh NWR, OR
1024	Big Boggy NWR, TX
1025	Massasoit NWR, MA
1026	Crystal River NWR, FL
1027	Tehama-Colusa Fish Facility, CA
1028	Pierce NWR, WA
1029	Harbor Island NWR, MI
1030	Ash Meadows NWR, NV
1031	Alligator River NWR, NC
1032	Eastern Shore of Virginia NWR, VA
1034	San Simeon Field Station, CA
1035	Sandy Point NWR, VI
1036	Currituck NWR, NC
1037	Kilauea Point NWR, HI
1038	Buenos Aires NWR, AZ
1039	Stewart B. McKinney NWR, CT
1040	Chickasaw NWR, TN
1042	Bitter Creek NWR, CA
1043	Willow Creek-Lurline WMA, CA
1044	Coachella Valley NWR, CA
1046	Hakalau Forest NWR, HI
1051	Cache River NWR, AR
1052	Steigerwald Lake NWR, WA
1053	Ozark Plateau NWR, OK
1054	Atchafalaya NWR, LA
1056	Little River NWR, OK
1057	John Hay NWR, NH
1060	Little Sandy NWR, TX
1062	Pilot Knob NWR, MO
1063	San Joaquin River NWR, CA
1065	Midway Atoll NWR (Hawaii Inset)
1066	Lake Ophelia NWR, LA
1075	McCall NFH, ID
1076	Sweetwater Marsh NWR, CA
1078	Sunkhaze Meadows NWR, ME
1084	Cameron Prairie NWR, LA
1091	Logan Cave NWR, AR
1092	Florida Panther NWR, FL
1093	Cape May NWR, NJ
1094	Pettaquamscutt Cove NWR, RI
1113	Laguna Cartagena NWR, PR
1118	Sacramento River NWR, CA
1119	Bond Swamp NWR, GA
1122	St Catherine Creek NWR, MS
1124	Bayou Sauvage NWR, LA
1125	Pocosin Lakes NWR, NC
1126	Lyons Ferry NFH, WA
1127	Sawtooth NFH, ID
1129	Driftless Area NWR, IA
1132	Cypress Creek NWR, IL
1137	Grand Bay NWR, AL & MS
1138	Hamden Slough NWR, MN
1139	Roanoke River NWR, NC
1140	Ace Basin NWR, SC
1142	Franz Lake NWR, WA
1143	Grays Harbor NWR, WA
1149	Ohio River Islands NWR, KY, PA & WV
1153	James River NWR, VA
1154	Dahomey NWR, MS
1155	Tallahatchie NWR, MS
1156	Tucannon NFH, WA
1158	Nestucca Bay NWR, OR
1159	Neal Smith NWR, IA
1160	Archie Carr NWR, FL
1165	Nisqually NFH, WA
1171	Ozark Cavefish NWR, MO
1174	Wallkill River NWR, NJ & NY
1175	North Central Valley WMA, CA
1178	Rydell NWR, MN
1179	Balcones Canyonlands NWR, TX
1180	Bayou Cocodrie NWR, LA
1181	Marin Islands NWR, CA
1182	Mortenson Lake NWR, WY
1183	Grand Cote NWR, LA
1184	Mora NWR, NM
	Siletz Bay NWR, OR
1185	Two Ponds NWR, CO
1186	Marais Des Cygnes NWR, KS
1187	Great Bay NWR, NH
1189	Lake Umbagog NWR, ME & NH
1190	Tualatin River NWR, OR
1193	Handy Brake NWR, LA
1196	Kealia Pond NWR, HI
1199	Bill Williams NWR, AZ
1200	Leslie Canyon NWR, AZ
1207	Crane Meadows NWR, MN
1208	Guam NWR (Pacific Area Inset)
1209	Bald Knob NWR, AR
1210	Deep Fork NWR, OK
1212	Emiquon NWR, IL
1213	Cokeville Meadows NWR, WY
1216	Trinity River NWR, TX
1218	Lake Wales Ridge NWR, FL
1224	Canaan Valley NWR, WV
1225	Pond Creek NWR, AR
	Patoka River NWR, IN
1229	Rocky Mountain Arsenal NWR, CO
1231	Big Branch Marsh NWR, LA
1232	Stone Lakes NWR, CA
1235	Big Muddy Nat. Fish & Wildlife Refuge, MO
1241	Mashpee NWR, MA
1244	Rappahannock R. NWR, VA
1245	San Diego NWR, CA
1247	Mandalay NWR, LA
1250	Ouray NFH, UT
1258	Ten Thousand Islands NWR, FL
1259	Key Cave NWR, AL
1261	Black Bayou Lake NWR, LA
1262	Boyer Chute NWR, NE
1267	Silvio O. Conte Nat. Fish & Wild. Ref., MA, NH & VT
1268	Waccamaw NWR, SC
1269	Magic Valley Hatchery, ID
1270	Eagle (Fish) Lab, ID
1271	Blackfoot Valley WMA, MT
1272	Clarks River NWR, KY
1274	Dworshak NFH, ID
1275	Livingston Stone NFH, CA
1276	Irrigon Fish Hatchery & Satellites, OR
1277	Lookingglass Fish Hatchery, WA
1278	Aroostook NWR, ME
1279	Colorado River WMA, UT
1280	Lost Trail NWR, MT
1281	Navassa Island NWR, BQ
1282	Shawangunk Grasslands NWR, NY
1283	Whittlesey Creek NWR, WI
1284	Port Louisa NWR, IA & IL
1285	Great River NWR, IL & MO
1286	Two Rivers NWR, IL & MO
1287	Middle Mississippi River NWR, IL & MO
1288	Big Oak NWR, IN
1289	Cat Island NWR, LA
1290	John W. & Louise Seier NWR, NE
1291	Guadalupe-Nipomo Dunes NWR, CA
1292	North Dakota NWR, ND
1293	Clearwater NFH, ID
1295	Northern Tallgrass Prairie NWR, MN
1296	Coldwater River NWR, MS
1297	Oahu Forest NWR, HI
1298	Caddo Lake NWR, TX
1299	Palmyra Atoll NWR (Pacific Area Inset)
1300	Kingman Reef NWR (Pacific Area Inset)
1301	Assabet NWR, MA
1302	Vieques NWR, PR
1303	Dakota Tallgrass Prairie, ND & SD
1309	Bayou Teche NWR, LA
1311	Red River NWR, LA
1312	Cahaba River NWR, AL

UNITED STATES
DEPARTMENT OF THE INTERIOR

NATIONAL FISH AND WILDLIFE MANAGEMENT AREAS

★ REGIONAL OFFICE   ━━━ REGIONAL BOUNDARY

UNITED STATES
FISH AND WILDLIFE SERVICE

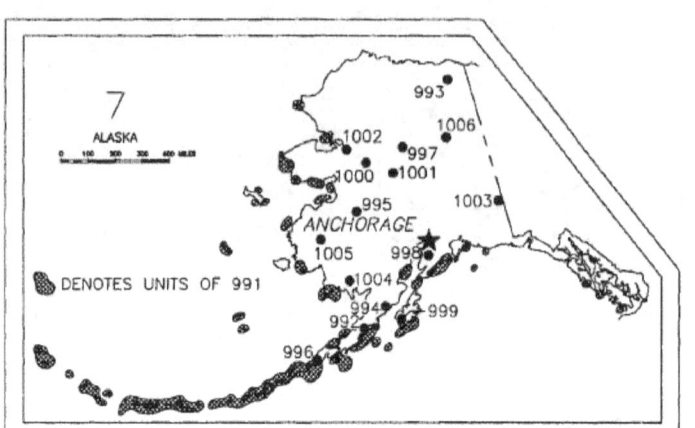

⊛ • NATIONAL WILDLIFE REFUGE
○ WILDLIFE RESEARCH CENTER
▲ NATIONAL FISH HATCHERY
▲ FISH HATCHERY AND RESEARCH STATION
△ FISHERY RESEARCH STATION
▲ FISH HATCHERY (REALTY INTEREST ONLY)

COMPILED IN THE DIVISION OF REALTY
WASHINGTON, DC SEPTEMBER 30, 2002

UNITED STATES
DEPARTMENT OF THE INTERIOR

NATIONAL FISH AND WILDLIFE MANAGEMENT AREAS

REGIONAL OFFICE ■■■■ REGIONAL BOUNDARY

UNITED STATES
FISH AND WILDLIFE SERVICE

●● NATIONAL WILDLIFE REFUGE
○ WILDLIFE RESEARCH CENTER
▲ NATIONAL FISH HATCHERY
▲ FISH HATCHERY AND RESEARCH STATION
△ FISHERY RESEARCH STATION
▲ FISH HATCHERY (REALTY INTEREST ONLY)

COMPILED IN THE DIVISION OF REALTY
WASHINGTON, DC SEPTEMBER 30, 2002

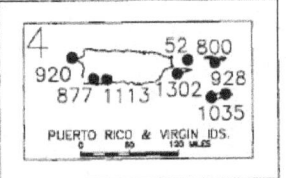

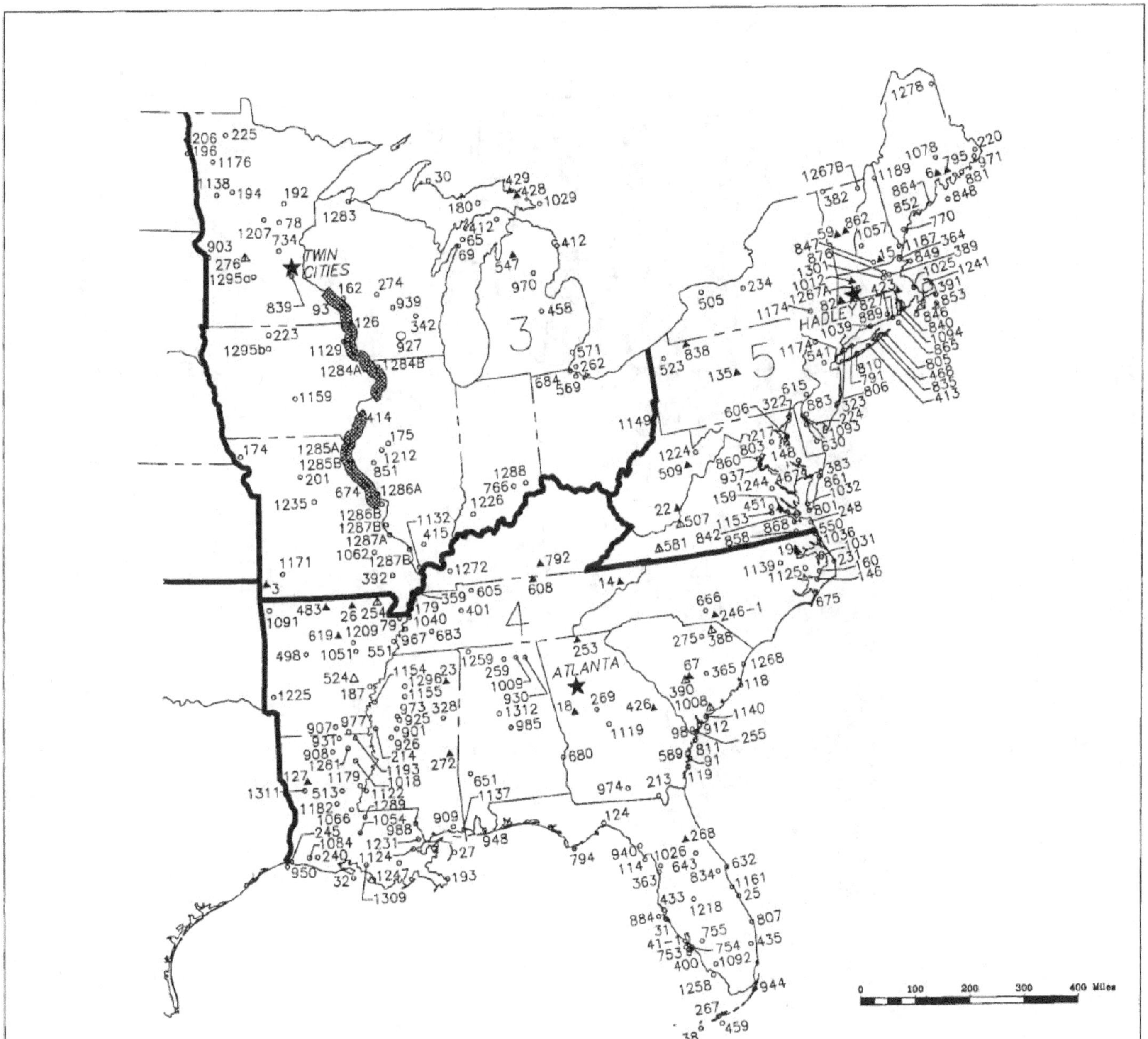

PUERTO RICO & VIRGIN IDS.

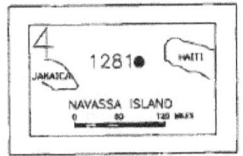

NAVASSA ISLAND

WATERFOWL PRODUCTION AREAS

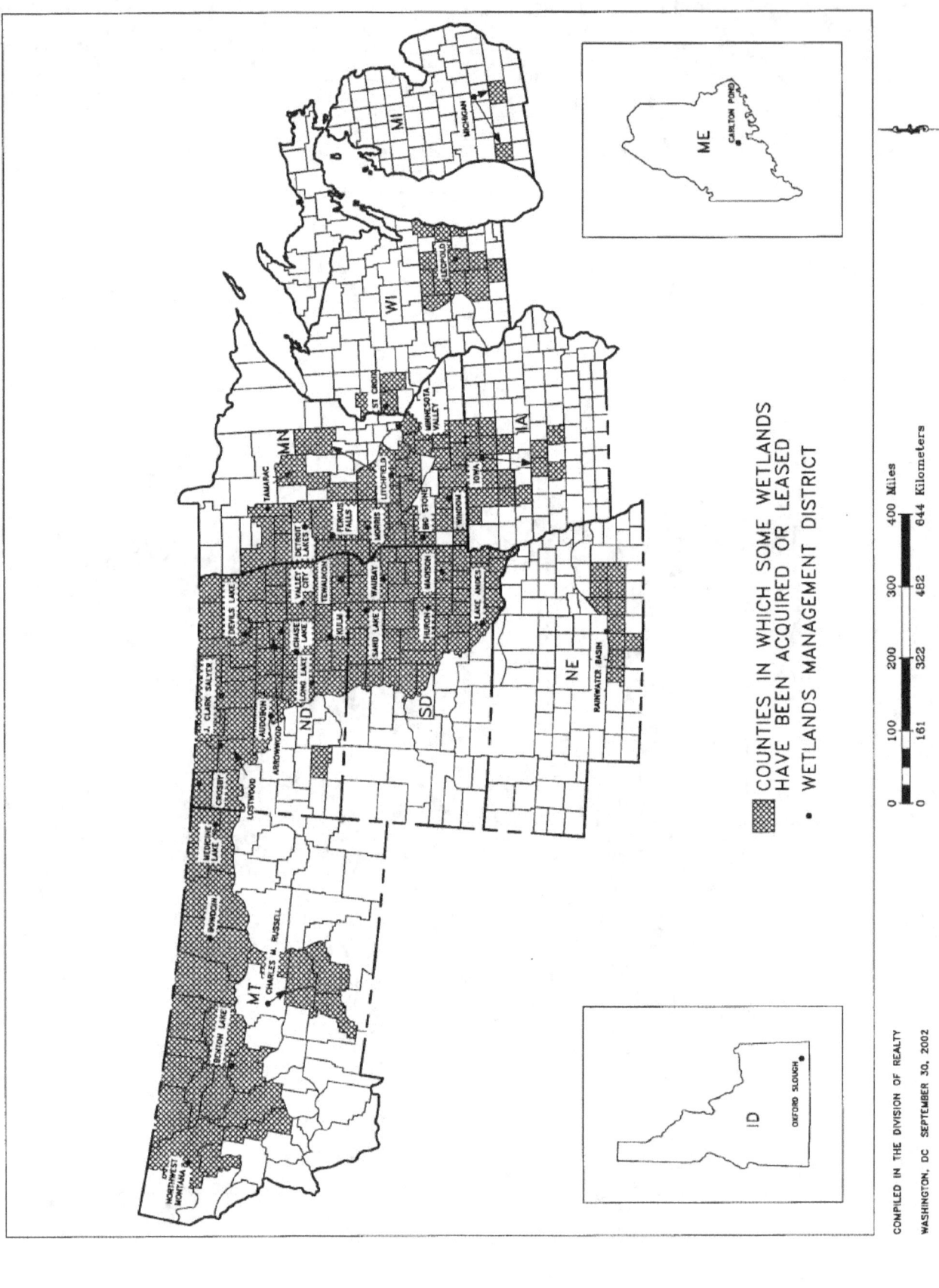

COUNTIES IN WHICH SOME WETLANDS
HAVE BEEN ACQUIRED OR LEASED

• WETLANDS MANAGEMENT DISTRICT

0	100	200	300	400 Miles
0	161	322	482	644 Kilometers

COMPILED IN THE DIVISION OF REALTY

WASHINGTON, DC   SEPTEMBER 30, 2002

Significant Land Acquisition Accomplishments in Fiscal Year 2002

The U.S. Fish and Wildlife Service acquired fee title or other interest in nearly 234,000 acres of land in Fiscal Year 2002, and the number of national wildlife refuges increased from 537 in FY 2001 to 540 during FY 2002. Although four new refuge units were established as part of the National Wildlife Refuge System (NWRS)—the Detroit River International Wildlife Refuge (IWR) in Michigan, Bayou Teche National Wildlife Refuge (NWR) in Louisiana, the Red River NWR in Louisiana, and the Cahaba River NWR in Alabama—the Wyandotte NWR was renamed and became a part of the Detroit River IWR. Therefore, there was a net increase of three refuges. It should also be noted that the acquisition boundary of the Northern Tallgrass Prairie NWR in Minnesota was extended into the State of Iowa, and Waseca County in Minnesota was added as the 203rd Waterfowl Production Area (WPA) County.

The remaining acreage at the New London National Fish Hatchery (NFH) was transferred to the State of Minnesota, and the lease on tribal lands for the Mescalero NFH was terminated (also see Notes section). These hatcheries no longer appear in this report (also see Notes section).

Detroit River IWR: Public Law 107-91, signed by the President on December 21, 2001, establishes the Detroit River International Wildlife Refuge. The new refuge is located in the area of the Lower Detroit River, downstream from the confluence of the Rouge River to the mouth of Lake Erie, in the State of Michigan. The Detroit River is an international waterway that flows through a metropolitan region of over five million people. Originally the river had extensive marshes along its banks and expansive upland habitat supporting abundant wildlife. It is estimated that 95 percent of the original wetlands were lost due to development. The Act authorizes the Fish and Wildlife Service to acquire lands and other interests within the new boundary that encompasses land around the Detroit River. The existing 327-acre

Wyandotte NWR is included in the boundary and is renamed the Detroit River International Wildlife Refuge. The Act encourages cooperative agreements for managing the lands that remain in state, local or private ownership, and provides for a study of the north reach of the Detroit River for potential future inclusion of fish and wildlife habitats and aquatic communities in the refuge.

Bayou Teche NWR: Established to protect, preserve and restore habitat for the Louisiana black bear population in St. Mary Parish, the Bayou Teche National Wildlife Refuge is the newest addition in the Louisiana Black Bear Project that also includes Bayou Cocodrie and Tensas River NWRs. The Louisiana black bear was federally listed as a threatened species in 1992. Both the Black Bear Conservation Committee, made up of representatives from over 50 agencies and organizations, and the Service prepared a restoration or recovery plan for the bear that includes the Bayou Teche habitat. This refuge represents the historic habitat of the only Louisiana black bear population that previously had no public land for a habitat base. These wooded areas that link the existing bear populations are important for ensuring the genetic variation necessary for the bears' long-term survival. The woodlands also offer a diverse habitat that is used by migratory waterfowl and other forms of terrestrial and aquatic life. The area is the first landfall for many neotropical birds after their flight across the Gulf of Mexico.

Red River NWR: Public Law 106-300 authorizes the establishment of the Red River National Wildlife Refuge in the area of Louisiana known as the Red River Valley, located along the Red River Waterway in Caddo, Bossier, Red River, Natchitoches, and De Soto Parishes. The refuge is established to protect and restore wetland habitats that will support migratory and non-migratory birds and other wildlife associated with the river basin ecosystems. The refuge will provide habitat and sanctuary for over 350 species of birds, including migratory and resident waterfowl, shore birds, and neotropical migratory birds. Reforestation and restoration of the native habitats will benefit a wide array of species. The refuge also offers recreational, research, and educational opportunities. The refuge lands, along with privately owned lands in the Red River Valley, will play an important role in the restoration of this ecosystem.

Cahaba River NWR (also see cover): Public Law 106-331 authorizes the establishment of the Cahaba River National Wildlife Refuge in Bibb County, Alabama. The refuge is located about five miles west of the City of Blockton, just north of the confluence of the Little Cahaba and Cahaba Rivers. This section of the river is extremely rich in species biodiversity and contains an extensive series of shoals vegetated with the Cahaba lily and waterwillow. Both sides of the river are forested with loblolly, longleaf pine and upland hardwoods. The refuge was established in the Cahaba River watershed to protect species of rare and imperiled fish and mollusks, such as the Cahaba shiner, goldline darter, round rocksnail, and cylindrical liopax. It also protects one candidate plant species and one plant species of concern. In addition, the refuge supports populations of resident game such as white-tailed deer, wild turkey, gray squirrels, and wood ducks.

Waseca County WPA: Administered as part of the Minnesota Valley Wetland Management District in Minnesota, Waseca County became the 203rd Waterfowl Production Area county within which fee or less-than-fee interests in small wetlands can be acquired for waterfowl production.

Also, there were several major additions to our existing national wildlife refuges. A 21,378-acre tract on South Padre Island near Brownsville, Texas, was acquired from The Nature Conservancy and added to the **Laguna Atascosa NWR.** This is a staging area for peregrine falcons in the spring and fall, and it is an important wintering area for the endangered piping plovers. It also provides excellent habitat for snowy plovers and other shorebird species. The Peregrine Fund and others began releasing endangered aplomado falcons in the project area with the goal of reestablishing a self-sustaining population there. In the last few years the Atlantic ridley sea turtles began nesting in small numbers on the Gulf side of the Island.

A total of 33,805 acres on the **Alaska Peninsula NWR** were acquired through donation. This tract was acquired with funds from the Mellon Foundation with the assistance of The Conservation Fund (TCF). These lands are located on both sides of the mouth of Morzhovoi Bay. The nearest villages are Cold Bay, located about 15 miles northeast, and False Pass, about the same distance southwest. Morzhovoi Bay, at the southern end of the Alaska Peninsula provides habitat for important species of water birds and land mammals, and these wetlands are recognized as *Wetlands of International Importance*. The entire populations of Pacific flyway brant and emperor geese, as well as the threatened Steller's eider rely on the abundance of nutrient-rich foods found at the Izembek Refuge. Resident tundra swans, numerous species of ducks, and over 20 species of shorebirds forage on the Refuge. Caribou use the Morzhovoi Bay area as winter range and an important migration corridor. Predators, such as brown bears, wolves, and wolverines are attracted to the abundance of prey species in the area. As a result of this and a previous donation, Morzhovoi Bay is now protected in the National Wildlife Refuge System.

The Service also completed the acquisition of lands located on the extreme northern portion of the **Kenai NWR.** These 4,247 acres are within the Kenai Wilderness Area. The lands are referred to as Point Possession as this was the site where Captain James Cook came ashore and claimed the Alaskan Territory in the name of the King of England during his quest for the Northwest Passage. The lands lie directly across the Turnagain Arm of Cook Inlet and are visible from the City of Anchorage.

The **Canaan Valley NWR** was established in 1994 to preserve the unique plant and wildlife communities of the nationally significant Blackwater River wetlands and to perpetuate migratory birds, threatened, and endangered species. This year's 11,953-acre acquisition increased the refuge to 15,245 acres. The addition preserves 4,600 acres of the largest high elevation wetlands east of the Rocky Mountains. The valley has one of the largest shrub swamps and the fourth largest bog in the eastern United States. The climate supports a relict boreal ecosystem which includes at least 580 species of plants, 109 of which have distinctly northern ranges. Fifty-two

plant species and 16 animal species, listed as species of concern by the State of West Virginia Division of Natural Resources, are known or thought to occur on the property. Canaan Valley offers important staging habitat for the American woodcock and contains a large breeding population. The refuge supports populations of the threatened Cheat mountain salamander and endangered West Virginia northern flying squirrel. Threatened bald eagles use the valley in the winter. Endangered Indiana bats may forage and/or roost in the valley during the summer months.

The acquisition of approximately 6,200 acres in partnership with the Trust for Public Lands/Hancock Timber Resource Group increases the size of the **Lake Umbagog NWR** to over 16,000 acres. The new acreage includes maple and birch upland forest, spruce bog, and a large emergent marsh. In addition to protecting critical wetlands, this acquisition links together many of the previously acquired refuge holdings and also provides significantly improved public access. One of New Hampshire's most wild and scenic lakes, Lake Umbagog and the surrounding wetlands support enormous concentrations of wildlife including waterfowl, songbirds, loons, osprey, bald eagles, and moose.

The Centennial Valley Conservation Easement Program in Beaverhead and Madison Counties, Montana, protects and provides an additional vital habitat corridor between the **Red Rock Lakes NWR,** the surrounding National Forest and Bureau of Land Management lands, The Nature Conservancy conservation easements, and the Partners for Wildlife projects. The acquisition of 6,146 acres of easements by the Service in FY 2002 complements the other activities undertaken by The Nature Conservancy, the Montana Land Reliance, and the Montana Department of Fish, Wildlife and Parks. The project area is within a watershed of the Upper Red Rock River ecosystem. There are 24 plant and animal species of special concern in the Centennial Valley.

There are a number of inholdings within the **Charles M. Russell NWR** in northeastern Montana. During the fiscal year, the Service acquired 2,740 acres from the Rocky Mountain Elk Foundation. This refuge includes wilderness, national historic sites, wild and scenic river segments, habitat for endangered and threatened species, and migratory bird and resident species habitat. The refuge also provides habitat and release sites for the endangered black-footed ferret and protection for the endangered pallid sturgeon. Acquisitions at CMR are coordinated with the Montana Fish, Wildlife and Parks Department.

San Joaquin River NWR currently consists of 13,117 acres of sloughs, lakes, seasonally flooded wetlands, grasslands, pasture, cropland, and riparian habitat. The Service in cooperation with the State of California was able to secure $7,000,000 in grant monies to put toward completion of the 4,040-acre acquisition of Mapes Ranch. The Mapes Ranch comprises over 50 percent of the entire refuge boundary. To date the Service has fee and easement interests in almost 9,724 acres of valuable wildlife habitat.

A significant inholding of 1,298 acres was acquired at the **Great Dismal Swamp NWR**. The Service has been working with the landowners since the 1970s. This tract contains unfragmented habitat which collectively provides protected feeding and breeding areas for black bear, turkey, great blue heron, neotropical migratory birds, wood ducks, and amphibians and reptiles such as the canebrake rattlesnake.

A complete list of new additions to the National Wildlife Refuge System is as follows:

State	Unit Name	Acres	Date Est.
Alabama	Cahaba River NWR	1,120	09/25/02
Louisiana	Bayou Teche NWR	9,074	10/31/01
Louisiana	Red River NWR	3,857	08/22/02
Michigan	Detroit River IWR	326	12/21/01
Minnesota	Waseca County WPA	249	02/07/02

TABLE 1 - SUMMARY BY CATEGORIES

CATEGORY		RESERVED FROM PUBLIC DOMAIN		ACQUIRED BY OTHER FEDERAL AGENCY		DEVISE OR GIFT	PURCHASED		AGREEMENT EASEMENT OR LEASE	TOTAL ACRES
		SOLE OR PRIMARY	SECONDARY	SOLE OR PRIMARY	SECONDARY		ACRES	COST ($)		
NATIONAL WILDLIFE REFUGES	540	81,301,616.64	713,174.61	3,115,807.54	941,661.35	703,140.82	4,054,794.60	1,662,780,890.69	1,275,885.82	92,104,081.38
WATERFOWL PRODUCTION AREAS	203	15,897.64	0.00	26,766.89	0.00	11,768.32	681,127.29	187,198,559.07	2,204,030.28	2,939,590.42
COORDINATION AREAS	50	56,586.61	0.00	139,342.97	55,739.14	0.00	681.13	13,480.00	65,544.00	315,893.85
TOTAL	793	81,374,100.89	713,174.61	3,281,917.40	997,400.49	714,909.14	4,736,603.02	1,849,992,929.76	3,541,460.10	95,359,565.65
ADMINISTRATIVE SITES	48	49.95	0.00	7.40	0.00	36.75	1,025.15	10,570,271.05	48.04	1,167.29
NATIONAL FISH HATCHERIES	69	3,607.09	987.09	2,596.85	3,682.01	1,337.18	4,932.17	2,750,204.59	4,361.78	21,504.17
TOTAL	117	3,657.04	987.09	2,604.25	3,682.01	1,373.93	5,957.32	13,320,475.64	4,409.82	22,671.46
GRAND TOTAL	910	81,377,757.93	714,161.70	3,284,521.65	1,001,082.50	716,283.07	4,742,560.34	1,863,313,405.40	3,545,869.92	95,382,237.11

REPORT DEFINITIONS

THE FOLLOWING DEFINITIONS ARE USED SOLELY FOR ADMINISTRATIVE PURPOSES IN GROUPING LAND USE CATEGORIES FOR THIS REPORT AND DO NOT NECESSARILY REFLECT THE DEFINITIONS FOUND IN 50 CFR 25.12

ADMINISTRATIVE SITE: LAND USED TO SUPPORT ADMINISTRATIVE PROGRAMS, SUCH AS MAINTENANCE FACILITIES OR OFFICES, AND OFF-SITE VISITOR CENTERS (TABLE 6)

COORDINATION AREA: ANY AREA ADMINISTRATED AS PART OF THE NATIONAL WILDLIFE REFUGE SYSTEM AND MANAGED BY THE STATE UNDER COOPERATIVE AGREEMENTS BETWEEN THE SERVICE AND A STATE FISH AND WILDLIFE AGENCY (TABLE 5).

MIGRATORY WATERFOWL REFUGE ON A FEDERAL WATER RESOURCE PROJECT: FEDERAL LAND MANAGED BY THE SERVICE AS PART OF THE NATIONAL WILDLIFE REFUGE SYSTEM TO MITIGATE A FEDERAL WATER RESOURCE PROJECT FOR THE BENEFIT OF MIGRATING WATERFOWL (AND OTHER WILDLIFE) UNDER THE FISH AND WILDLIFE COORDINATION ACT (TABLE 9).

NATIONAL FISH HATCHERY: FACILITY WHERE FISH ARE RAISED. HATCHERY OBJECTIVES ARE TO REPLENISH DEPLETED STOCKS, TO MITIGATE FEDERAL WATER PROJECTS, TO ASSIST WITH THE MANAGEMENT OF FISHERY RESOURCES ON FEDERAL (PRIMARILY SERVICE) AND INDIAN LANDS, AND TO ENHANCE RECREATIONAL FISHERIES (TABLE 7.)

NATIONAL WILDLIFE REFUGE: ANY AREA OF THE NATIONAL WILDLIFE REFUGE SYSTEM, EXCEPT COORDINATION AREAS AND WATERFOWL PRODUCTION AREAS (TABLE 3).

WATERFOWL PRODUCTION AREA: ANY WETLAND OR POTHOLE AREA ACQUIRED PURSUANT TO THE MIGRATORY BIRD HUNTING AND CONSERVATION STAMP ACT OR OTHER STATUTORY AUTHORITY AND ADMINISTERED AS PART OF THE NATIONAL WILDLIFE REFUGE SYSTEMS AND IDENTIFIED BY COUNTY DESIGNATION (TABLE 4).

WILDERNESS AREA: SERVICE LAND DESIGNATED BY CONGRESS TO BE MANAGED AS A UNIT OF THE NATIONAL WILDERNESS PRESERVATION SYSTEM, IN ACCORDANCE WITH THE TERMS OF THE WILDERNESS ACT OF 1964. ALL SERVICE WILDERNESS AREAS OCCUR WITHIN NATIONAL WILDLIFE REFUGES, WITH THE EXCEPTION OF MOUNT MASSIVE WILDERNESS AREA WHICH IS LOCATED AT THE LEADVILLE NATIONAL FISH HATCHERY (TABLE 8).

NOTE: FOR CONVERSION TO METRIC UNITS

1 ACRE = .405 HECTARES

TABLE 2 - SUMMARY BY STATES, ASSOCIATED GOVERNMENTS AND POSSESSIONS

STATE		RESERVED FROM PUBLIC DOMAIN		ACQUIRED BY OTHER FEDERAL AGENCY		DEVISE OR GIFT	PURCHASED		AGREEMENT EASEMENT OR LEASE	TOTAL ACRES
		SOLE OR PRIMARY	SECONDARY	SOLE OR PRIMARY	SECONDARY		ACRES	COST ($)		
ALABAMA	10	0.00	0.00	8,322.98	37,821.62	1,214.59	10,850.91	25,052,957.00	1,317.69	59,527.79
ALASKA	49	76,243,205.75	66,651.00	1.89	0.00	43,221.98	275,455.23	125,386,511.65	145,693.53	76,774,229.38
ARIZONA	15	1,548,669.60	27,270.45	4,212.93	12,501.23	1,200.00	123,818.50	17,415,217.00	8,606.91	1,726,279.62
ARKANSAS	13	8,881.60	0.00	163,974.36	823.77	3,841.20	183,098.78	64,354,626.98	711.40	361,331.11
CALIFORNIA	42	81,073.38	67,454.86	35,380.77	6,467.84	9,687.99	149,667.59	186,334,375.06	122,605.16	472,337.59
COLORADO	11	16,602.00	0.00	963.21	17,000.00	90.43	48,227.72	13,405,978.36	1,766.07	84,649.43
CONNECTICUT	1	0.00	0.00	0.00	4.90	243.79	621.93	15,753,590.00	1.72	872.34
DELAWARE	2	0.00	0.00	541.50	0.00	29.60	24,602.16	7,856,752.76	953.19	26,126.45
FLORIDA	30	4,853.76	154.00	32,609.64	138,262.70	4,386.68	247,072.41	123,561,105.45	550,657.60	977,996.79
GEORGIA	10	0.00	0.00	39,373.66	3,275.80	25,579.36	408,365.39	8,856,027.04	4,039.33	480,633.54
HAWAII	13	254,418.10	0.00	72.80	61.15	91.38	43,791.46	38,574,518.60	945.55	299,380.44
IDAHO	15	26,624.92	26,758.15	1,125.46	1,070.32	181.26	20,787.51	3,657,832.86	15,617.48	92,165.10
ILLINOIS	11	65.15	0.00	43,165.64	60,719.81	3,912.29	31,962.97	17,449,675.94	409.82	140,235.68
INDIANA	3	0.00	0.00	219.03	51,000.00	412.58	12,981.88	7,906,192.60	0.00	64,613.49
IOWA	27	333.66	0.00	0.00	47,257.94	81.22	64,428.70	36,671,425.96	712.01	112,793.53
KANSAS	5	0.00	0.00	116.50	29,241.21	199.20	29,131.77	5,573,019.40	6.37	58,695.05
KENTUCKY	3	0.00	0.00	0.00	20.47	0.00	9,057.81	6,525,841.15	0.00	9,078.28
LOUISIANA	24	10,462.65	2,892.30	251,417.20	0.00	16,577.79	247,748.04	109,764,582.16	16,353.95	545,451.93
MAINE	12	0.00	0.00	11,536.27	0.00	4,252.99	44,856.99	30,921,517.02	734.82	61,381.07
MARYLAND	5	0.00	0.00	11,855.89	0.00	3,940.59	29,165.62	14,823,503.23	68.21	45,030.31
MASSACHUSETTS	12	0.00	0.00	4,454.53	0.00	720.69	11,539.95	17,824,348.74	81.58	16,796.75
MICHIGAN	13	2,999.51	121.70	7,506.64	1,653.32	424.25	102,187.51	6,589,041.02	351.00	115,243.93
MINNESOTA	59	288.18	0.00	164,451.26	15,674.97	3,679.43	287,920.03	97,157,483.08	75,407.54	547,421.41
MISSISSIPPI	12	40.08	0.00	72,576.62	7,070.45	4,979.21	130,879.37	77,478,243.03	10,493.60	226,039.33
MISSOURI	12	0.00	0.00	11,087.58	13,607.00	90.00	45,814.99	7,780,809.42	259.43	70,859.00
MONTANA	53	433,134.99	388,952.77	96,735.26	155,325.01	6,550.57	90,246.27	21,134,716.08	157,528.48	1,328,473.35
NEBRASKA	17	15,786.88	2,684.81	70,015.85	0.00	4,781.65	81,719.87	16,221,546.74	3,341.89	178,330.95
NEVADA	11	2,218,410.57	18,261.22	0.00	623.20	2,539.11	85,817.81	22,976,078.25	63,964.22	2,389,616.13
NEW HAMPSHIRE	5	0.00	0.00	1,054.00	0.00	1,836.60	12,896.18	10,223,063.96	35.21	15,821.99
NEW JERSEY	4	0.00	0.00	6.86	1.96	4,025.79	64,256.86	104,214,144.10	2,905.35	71,196.82
NEW MEXICO	10	15,766.26	57,215.48	0.00	438.52	220,200.00	90,697.08	5,317,666.69	734.60	385,051.89
NEW YORK	12	0.00	0.00	1,829.19	0.00	5,624.04	19,681.25	10,345,319.67	1,946.95	29,081.43
NORTH CAROLINA	12	0.00	0.00	50,964.86	11.38	237,752.65	125,378.66	32,878,903.52	9,840.30	423,947.85
NORTH DAKOTA	108	18,537.86	0.00	138,434.97	14,962.69	4,333.98	318,787.45	29,174,186.86	1,070,969.53	1,566,026.48
OHIO	3	77.13	0.00	0.00	0.00	2,445.42	5,754.14	3,931,593.55	598.20	8,874.89
OKLAHOMA	10	77,966.20	0.00	622.49	61,224.08	450.55	25,906.49	13,477,664.31	3,861.89	170,031.70
OREGON	28	267,494.20	4,608.28	63,243.93	9,826.80	1,379.52	225,251.20	43,827,403.30	786.47	572,590.40
PENNSYLVANIA	4	0.00	0.00	87.26	45.04	243.14	9,672.39	9,855,576.75	0.00	10,047.83
RHODE ISLAND	5	0.00	0.00	581.96	0.00	630.89	810.16	15,369,500.00	156.20	2,179.21
SOUTH CAROLINA	9	0.00	0.00	55,214.67	100.00	8,862.73	54,865.19	19,816,578.22	43,915.16	162,957.75
SOUTH DAKOTA	51	1,848.76	0.00	28,782.89	581.00	7,969.75	163,612.51	29,398,902.79	1,097,669.97	1,300,464.88
TENNESSEE	8	0.00	0.00	7,925.87	53,310.81	8.26	40,038.97	31,808,628.19	15,682.07	116,965.98
TEXAS	22	0.00	0.00	40,742.73	19,811.86	13,741.64	394,709.41	172,856,736.43	65,313.11	534,318.76
UTAH	9	65,780.81	0.00	2,382.91	0.00	4,272.21	34,675.44	3,468,528.72	4,917.28	112,028.65
VERMONT	4	0.00	0.00	0.00	0.00	346.36	32,797.82	7,325,897.37	86.00	33,230.18
VIRGINIA	14	0.00	0.00	5,994.33	0.00	53,594.95	68,827.42	75,365,530.14	4,572.15	132,988.85
WASHINGTON	39	40,486.42	2,182.11	35,062.66	187,347.02	859.03	70,151.51	36,788,849.78	8,867.26	344,956.01
WEST VIRGINIA	4	0.00	0.00	18.90	0.00	166.87	18,381.08	42,934,380.56	28.34	18,595.19
WISCONSIN	26	747.93	0.00	99,468.37	40,341.00	174.64	95,700.33	20,454,897.32	37.76	236,470.03
WYOMING	15	23,201.58	11,501.57	16,079.93	13,549.63	4,474.22	26,095.73	11,080,200.76	6,954.47	101,857.13
AMERICAN SAMOA	1	0.00	37,453.00	1,613.00	0.00	0.00	0.00	0.00	0.00	39,066.00
BAKER ISLAND	1	0.00	0.00	31,736.89	0.00	0.00	0.00	0.00	0.00	31,736.89
GUAM	1	0.00	0.00	772.10	0.00	0.00	0.00	0.00	22,456.00	23,228.10

TABLE 2 - SUMMARY BY STATES, ASSOCIATED GOVERNMENTS AND POSSESSIONS

STATE		RESERVED FROM PUBLIC DOMAIN		ACQUIRED BY OTHER FEDERAL AGENCY		DEVISE OR GIFT	PURCHASED		AGREEMENT EASEMENT OR LEASE	TOTAL ACRES
		SOLE OR PRIMARY	SECONDARY	SOLE OR PRIMARY	SECONDARY		ACRES	COST ($)		
HOWLAND ISLAND	1	0.00	0.00	32,550.25	0.00	0.00	0.00	0.00	0.00	32,550.25
JARVIS ISLAND	1	0.00	0.00	37,519.17	0.00	0.00	0.00	0.00	0.00	37,519.17
JOHNSTON ATOLL	1	0.00	0.00	0.00	0.00	0.00	0.00	0.00	100.00	100.00
KINGMAN REEF	1	0.00	0.00	426,392.00	0.00	0.00	0.00	0.00	0.00	426,392.00
MIDWAY ISLANDS	1	0.00	0.00	298,362.30	0.00	0.00	0.00	0.00	0.00	298,362.30
NAVASSA ISLAND	1	0.00	0.00	364,950.00	0.00	0.00	0.00	0.00	0.00	364,950.00
PALMYRA ATOLL	1	0.00	0.00	504,576.00	0.00	0.00	0.00	0.00	0.00	504,576.00
PUERTO RICO	5	0.00	0.00	5,788.54	68.00	0.00	1,270.00	2,999,265.63	787.10	7,913.64
VIRGIN ISLANDS	3	0.00	0.00	45.15	0.00	0.00	525.94	3,382,470.00	0.00	571.09
GRAND TOTAL	910	81,377,757.93	714,161.70	3,284,521.65	1,001,082.50	716,283.07	4,742,560.34	1,863,313,405.40	3,545,869.92	95,382,237.11

STATE		RESERVED FROM PUBLIC DOMAIN		ACQUIRED BY OTHER FEDERAL AGENCY		DEVISE OR GIFT	PURCHASED		AGREEMENT EASEMENT OR LEASE	TOTAL ACRES
		SOLE OR PRIMARY	SECONDARY	SOLE OR PRIMARY	SECONDARY		ACRES	COST ($)		
ALABAMA	4	0.00	0.00	0.00	0.00	0.00	1,301.65	2,370,700.00	0.00	1,301.65
ALASKA	8	0.00	0.00	0.00	0.00	33,805.67	923.64	1,005,260.00	.11	34,730.17
ARIZONA	1	0.00	0.00	0.00	0.00	0.00	0.00	0.00	7,030.72	7,030.72
ARKANSAS	3	0.00	0.00	0.00	0.00	0.00	1,840.00	2,742,585.00	(131.26)	1,840.00
CALIFORNIA	7	0.00	0.00	0.00	0.00	61.17	740.20	3,757,768.66	1,303.12	2,104.49
COLORADO	3	0.00	0.00	0.00	0.00	0.00	611.61	191,000.00	(511.79)	711.11
CONNECTICUT	1	0.00	0.00	0.00	0.00	0.00	36.30	491,850.00	0.00	36.30
DELAWARE	1	0.00	0.00	0.00	0.00	0.00	108.45	835,000.00	0.00	108.45
FLORIDA	5	0.00	0.00	0.00	0.00	(107.44)	105.87	8,667,325.00	0.00	(1.57)
IDAHO	1	0.00	0.00	0.00	0.00	0.00	148.90	203,000.00	0.00	148.90
ILLINOIS	3	0.00	0.00	0.00	0.00	0.00	1,040.50	592,700.00	0.00	1,040.50
INDIANA	1	0.00	0.00	0.00	0.00	0.00	18.42	12,300.00	0.00	18.42
IOWA	9	0.00	0.00	0.00	0.00	0.00	2,308.78	4,236,863.04	0.00	2,308.78
LOUISIANA	9	0.00	0.00	0.00	0.00	0.00	14,728.20	7,345,740.00	2,280.00	17,860.71
MAINE	3	0.00	0.00	0.00	0.00	0.00	3,329.64	1,470,236.35	60.34	3,389.98
MARYLAND	2	0.00	0.00	0.00	0.00	0.00	238.51	926,396.62	.27	238.78
MASSACHUSETTS	3	0.00	0.00	0.00	0.00	0.00	167.12	1,705,937.00	0.00	167.12
MICHIGAN	1	0.00	0.00	0.00	0.00	0.00	(279.02)	0.00	0.00	(279.02)
MINNESOTA	23	0.00	0.00	0.00	0.00	20.74	2,287.02	2,179,126.32	1,637.20	3,944.96
MISSISSIPPI	7	0.00	0.00	0.00	0.00	80.00	921.41	1,454,451.00	0.00	1,001.41
MONTANA	15	0.00	0.00	0.00	0.00	7.85	3,109.00	1,518,400.00	15,661.73	18,778.58
NEBRASKA	4	0.00	0.00	(159.30)	0.00	163.00	543.22	453,900.00	(553.00)	546.92
NEVADA	3	0.00	0.00	0.00	0.00	0.00	1,971.86	2,060,832.00	0.00	1,971.86
NEW HAMPSHIRE	1	0.00	0.00	0.00	0.00	0.00	8,204.30	3,682,371.00	0.00	8,204.30
NEW JERSEY	3	0.00	0.00	0.00	0.00	46.29	445.29	5,988,089.33	.25	491.83
NEW YORK	1	0.00	0.00	0.00	0.00	0.00	74.79	69,495.00	0.00	74.79
NORTH CAROLINA	2	0.00	0.00	0.00	0.00	0.00	1,297.90	1,112,180.00	(3,950.08)	1,297.90
NORTH DAKOTA	19	0.00	0.00	0.00	0.00	0.00	625.02	336,760.00	34,348.88	34,991.90
OHIO	1	0.00	0.00	0.00	0.00	0.00	0.00	0.00	.05	.05
OKLAHOMA	2	0.00	0.00	0.00	0.00	0.00	1,108.35	880,815.00	0.00	1,108.35
OREGON	2	0.00	0.00	0.00	0.00	0.00	139.83	253,000.00	0.00	139.83
RHODE ISLAND	2	0.00	0.00	0.00	0.00	0.00	26.70	1,700,000.00	0.00	26.70
SOUTH CAROLINA	1	0.00	0.00	0.00	0.00	0.00	510.67	1,165,965.00	0.00	510.67
SOUTH DAKOTA	34	0.00	0.00	0.00	0.00	1,560.36	941.63	622,466.50	59,866.02	62,426.01
TENNESSEE	2	0.00	0.00	0.00	0.00	0.00	1,497.99	2,612,500.00	0.00	5,046.99
TEXAS	6	0.00	0.00	160.00	0.00	529.55	2,692.33	1,840,108.25	680.08	4,061.96
UTAH	2	0.00	0.00	0.00	0.00	0.00	0.00	0.00	0.00	0.00
VERMONT	1	0.00	0.00	0.00	0.00	0.00	263.44	227,500.00	0.00	263.44
VIRGINIA	2	0.00	0.00	0.00	0.00	0.00	484.54	4,853,984.00	0.00	484.54
WASHINGTON	5	0.00	0.00	0.00	0.00	19.50	941.29	3,341,000.00	80.30	1,041.09
WEST VIRGINIA	1	0.00	0.00	0.00	0.00	0.00	11,961.43	16,000,000.00	0.00	11,961.43
WISCONSIN	8	0.00	0.00	0.00	0.00	0.00	596.19	1,699,888.94	0.00	596.19
WYOMING	2	1,742.76	0.00	170.00	0.00	0.00	0.00	0.00	320.00	2,232.76
VIRGIN ISLANDS	1	0.00	0.00	0.00	0.00	0.00	.82	30,100.00	0.00	.82
GRAND TOTAL	215	1,742.76	0.00	170.70	0.00	36,186.69	68,013.79	90,610,594.01	118,142.94	233,960.77

TABLE 3 - NATIONAL WILDLIFE REFUGES

STATE AND UNIT	RESERVED FROM PUBLIC DOMAIN		ACQUIRED BY OTHER FEDERAL AGENCY		DEVISE OR GIFT	PURCHASED		AGREEMENT EASEMENT OR LEASE	TOTAL ACRES
	SOLE OR PRIMARY	SECONDARY	SOLE OR PRIMARY	SECONDARY		ACRES	COST ($)		
ALABAMA									
BON SECOUR	0.00	0.00	0.00	0.00	135.05	6,087.59	21,098,794.00	575.00	6,797.64
CAHABA RIVER	0.00	0.00	0.00	0.00	0.00	1,120.00	2,103,000.00	0.00	1,120.00
CHOCTAW	0.00	0.00	0.00	E 4,218.00	0.00	0.00	0.00	0.00	4,218.00
EUFAULA (1)	0.00	0.00	0.00	E 7,929.00	0.00	24.19	80,000.00	0.00	7,953.19
FERN CAVE	0.00	0.00	0.00	0.00	0.00	199.23	110,000.00	0.00	199.23
FSA INTEREST AL ** *	0.00	0.00	0.00	0.00	0.00	0.00	0.00	742.69	742.69
GRAND BAY (27)	0.00	0.00	0.00	0.00	895.86	1,822.00	710,613.00	0.00	2,717.86
KEY CAVE	0.00	0.00	0.00	0.00	0.00	1,060.00	0.00	0.00	1,060.00
SAUTA CAVE	0.00	0.00	0.00	0.00	0.00	264.00	575,000.00	0.00	264.00
WATERCRESS DARTER	0.00	0.00	0.00	0.00	0.00	24.52	250,850.00	0.00	24.52
WHEELER	0.00	0.00	8,322.98 T	25,674.62	183.68	249.38	149,700.00	0.00	34,430.66
STATE TOTAL 10	0.00	0.00	8,322.98	37,821.62	1,214.59	10,850.91	25,052,957.00	1,317.69	59,527.79
ALASKA									
ALASKA MARITIME	3,361,307.44 N	65,695.00	0.00	0.00	0.00	11,035.02	7,677,891.80	27,209.33	3,465,246.79
ALASKA PENINSULA	3,456,905.00	0.00	0.00	0.00	34,320.12	43,184.99	209,100.00	.34	3,534,410.45
ARCTIC	19,263,110.00 LM	0.00	0.00	0.00	0.00	22,812.00	0.00	.40	19,285,922.40
BECHAROF	1,200,000.00	0.00	0.00	0.00	0.00	17.75	204,300.00	0.00	1,200,017.75
INNOKO	3,850,000.00	0.00	0.00	0.00	0.00	319.99	196,500.00	1.22	3,850,321.21
IZEMBEK	302,201.00 N	893.00	0.00	0.00	7,981.78	0.00	0.00	0.00	311,075.78
KANUTI	1,430,000.00	0.00	0.00	0.00	0.00	159.91	68,000.00	0.00	1,430,159.91
KENAI	1,904,472.00	0.00	0.00	0.00	0.00	3,675.90	7,319,299.96	30.35	1,908,178.25
KODIAK	1,656,169.40	0.00	0.00	0.00	883.33	175,339.06	105,817,995.84	101,000.24	1,933,392.03
KOYUKUK	3,550,000.00	0.00	0.00	0.00	0.00	0.00	0.00	.53	3,550,000.53
NOWITNA	1,560,000.00	0.00	0.00	0.00	0.00	0.00	0.00	0.00	1,560,000.00
SELAWIK	2,150,000.00	0.00	0.00	0.00	0.00	0.00	0.00	2.01	2,150,002.01
TETLIN	700,000.00	0.00	0.00	0.00	0.00	5.00	15,500.00	53.54	700,058.54
TOGIAK	4,097,430.00	0.00	0.00	0.00	0.00	1,309.66	1,707,000.00	1.28	4,098,740.94
YUKON DELTA	19,131,581.00 BIA	63.00	0.00	0.00	0.00	17,093.00	0.00	17,357.48	19,166,094.48
YUKON FLATS	8,630,000.00	0.00	0.00	0.00	0.00	399.85	176,000.00	.53	8,630,400.38
STATE TOTAL 16	76,243,175.84	66,651.00	0.00	0.00	43,185.23	275,352.13	123,391,587.60	145,657.23	76,774,021.43
ARIZONA									
BILL WILLIAMS RIVER	2,781.00 R	943.07	0.00 R	756.00	0.00	1,574.69	1,600,000.00	0.00	6,054.76
BUENOS AIRES	0.00	0.00	0.00	0.00	0.00	116,512.99	13,705,291.00	1,462.77	117,775.76
CABEZA PRIETA	860,000.00	0.00	0.00	0.00	0.00	41.32	18,300.00	0.00	860,041.32
CIBOLA (2)	3,577.92	0.00	4,212.95 R	623.38	0.00	191.81	382,000.00	0.00	8,606.04
HAVASU (2)	10,004.54 R	10,418.30	0.00 R	9,816.98	0.00	40.00	8,000.00	0.00	30,279.82
IMPERIAL (2)	0.00 R	15,861.27	0.00 R	1,304.87	0.00	643.62	201,724.00	0.00	17,809.76
KOFA	665,400.00	0.00	0.00	0.00	0.00	1,080.00	396,000.00	0.00	666,480.00
LESLIE CANYON	0.00	0.00	0.00	0.00	1,200.00	1,564.76	250,000.00	7,030.72	9,795.48
SAN BERNARDINO	0.00	0.00	0.00	0.00	0.00	2,367.87	830,600.00	.70	2,368.57
STATE TOTAL 9	1,541,763.46	27,222.64	4,212.95	12,501.23	1,200.00	123,817.06	17,389,915.00	8,494.19	1,719,211.51
ARKANSAS									
BALD KNOB	0.00	0.00	0.00	0.00	0.00	14,759.95	9,182,000.00	0.00	14,759.95
BIG LAKE	8,875.60	0.00	1,597.34	0.00	0.00	562.91	31,854.69	.25	11,036.10
CACHE RIVER	0.00	0.00	6,091.19	0.00	787.12	50,080.92	37,419,678.42	0.00	56,959.23
FELSENTHAL	0.00	0.00	64,813.34	0.00	0.00	88.80	100,000.00	0.00	64,902.14
FSA INTEREST AR ** *	0.00	0.00	3,161.47	0.00	0.00	0.00	0.00	297.20	3,458.67
HOLLA BEND	0.00	0.00	4,068.00	0.00	28.85	2,201.45	339,903.00	.73	6,299.03
LOGAN CAVE	0.00	0.00	0.00	0.00	0.00	123.59	109,136.00	0.00	123.59
OVERFLOW	0.00	0.00	0.00	0.00	0.00	12,962.89	10,300,520.50	0.00	12,962.89
POND CREEK	0.00	0.00	0.00	E 700.00	1,933.11	24,182.70	0.00	0.00	26,815.81

TABLE 3 - NATIONAL WILDLIFE REFUGES

STATE AND UNIT	RESERVED FROM PUBLIC DOMAIN		ACQUIRED BY OTHER FEDERAL AGENCY		DEVISE OR GIFT	PURCHASED		AGREEMENT EASEMENT OR LEASE	TOTAL ACRES
	SOLE OR PRIMARY	SECONDARY	SOLE OR PRIMARY	SECONDARY		ACRES	COST ($)		
ARKANSAS									
WAPANOCCA	0.00	0.00	0.00	0.00	0.00	5,484.17	1,351,416.00	0.00	5,484.17
WHITE RIVER	6.00	0.00	84,243.02 E	45.80	1,092.12	72,614.56	5,464,193.37	413.22	158,414.72
STATE TOTAL 10	8,881.60	0.00	163,974.36	745.80	3,841.20	183,061.94	64,298,701.98	711.40	361,216.30
CALIFORNIA									
ANTIOCH DUNES	0.00	0.00	0.00	0.00	0.00	55.38	2,135,000.00	0.00	55.38
BITTER CREEK	0.00	0.00	0.00	0.00	40.00	14,056.70	4,779,600.00	0.00	14,096.70
BLUE RIDGE	0.00	0.00	0.00	0.00	0.00	897.08	642,500.00	0.00	897.08
BUTTE SINK	0.00	0.00	0.00	0.00	0.00	732.86	3,850,700.00	10,310.64	11,043.50
CASTLE ROCK	0.00	0.00	0.00	0.00	0.00	13.89	41,250.00	0.00	13.89
CIBOLA (3) *	1,255.00	0.00	2,094.52	0.00	600.00	0.00	0.00	297.00	4,246.52
CLEAR LAKE	0.00	R 33,440.00	13,020.07	0.00	0.00	0.00	0.00	0.00	46,460.07
COACHELLA VALLEY	0.00	0.00	0.00	0.00	1,029.51	2,548.10	9,313,908.77	0.00	3,577.61
COLUSA	0.00	0.00	0.00	0.00	0.00	4,039.71	291,280.85	.27	4,039.98
DELEVAN	0.00	0.00	0.00	0.00	0.00	5,796.54	2,345,739.00	0.00	5,796.54
DON EDWARDS SAN FRAN. BAY	0.00	0.00	37.26	0.00	449.34	19,601.16	35,716,134.00	2,301.98	22,389.74
ELLICOTT SLOUGH	0.00	0.00	0.00	0.00	0.00	164.44	971,000.00	35.11	199.55
FARALLON	91.00	CG 120.00	0.00	0.00	0.00	0.00	0.00	0.00	211.00
FSA INTEREST CA ** *	0.00	0.00	80.00	0.00	0.00	0.00	0.00	0.00	80.00
GRASSLANDS	0.00	0.00	0.00	0.00	0.00	13,064.85	13,811,228.00	67,479.07	80,543.92
GUADALUPE-NIPOMO DUNES	0.00	0.00	0.00	0.00	2,553.00	0.00	0.00	0.00	2,553.00
HAVASU (3) *	10.00	R 4,160.23	0.00	R 3,065.11	0.00	0.00	0.00	0.00	7,235.34
HOPPER MOUNTAIN	0.00	0.00	0.00	0.00	0.00	2,471.00	640,000.00	0.00	2,471.00
HUMBOLDT BAY	0.00	CG 1.00	0.00	0.00	485.48	2,425.24	5,244,610.00	0.00	2,911.72
IMPERIAL (3) *	0.00	R 6,309.05	0.00	R 1,649.14	0.00	0.00	0.00	0.00	7,958.19
KERN	0.00	0.00	0.00	0.00	0.00	10,618.17	579,912.00	0.00	10,618.17
LOWER KLAMATH (4)	39,315.72	0.00	0.00	0.00	447.89	4,530.53	3,390,123.00	0.00	44,294.14
MARIN ISLANDS	0.00	0.00	0.00	0.00	102.59	28.70	1,010,000.00	0.00	131.29
MERCED	0.00	0.00	0.00	0.00	0.00	3,803.82	2,180,000.00	1.76	3,805.58
MODOC	40.00	0.00	0.00	0.00	310.00	6,670.62	1,548,854.19	.61	7,021.23
NORTH CENTRAL VALLEY	0.00	0.00	0.00	0.00	0.00	586.63	1,565,531.00	6,543.76	7,130.39
PIXLEY	0.00	0.00	4,521.05	0.00	170.00	1,693.53	1,339,998.00	4.55	6,389.13
SACRAMENTO	0.00	0.00	0.00	0.00	0.00	10,785.34	162,998.00	0.00	10,785.34
SACRAMENTO RIVER	0.00	0.00	0.00	0.00	54.23	10,795.08	30,825,571.65	6,680.99	17,530.30
SALINAS RIVER	0.00	0.00	363.61	0.00	0.00	0.00	0.00	3.82	367.43
SAN DIEGO	0.00	0.00	88.00	0.00	2,371.16	5,352.06	21,181,920.00	2,201.01	10,012.23
SAN JOAQUIN RIVER	0.00	0.00	0.00	0.00	0.00	6,776.49	21,345,808.00	2,946.97	9,723.46
SAN LUIS	8.00	0.00	14,760.00	0.00	0.00	7,422.41	2,171,055.00	703.00	22,893.41
SAN PABLO BAY	0.00	0.00	0.00	0.00	248.72	1,741.00	6,742,600.00	11,200.00	13,189.72
SEAL BEACH	0.00	0.00	0.00	N 852.17	0.00	0.00	0.00	58.54	910.71
SONNY BONO SALTON SEA	0.00	R 23,424.58	360.98	0.00	0.00	9,342.14	294,461.80	4,531.17	37,658.87
STONE LAKES	0.00	0.00	0.00	0.00	510.27	627.99	4,113,089.00	1,705.56	2,843.82
SUTTER	0.00	0.00	0.00	0.00	0.00	2,590.16	291,281.80	0.00	2,590.16
SWEETWATER MARSH	0.00	0.00	0.00	0.00	315.80	0.00	0.00	0.00	315.80
TIJUANA SLOUGH	0.00	0.00	0.00	N 551.42	0.00	406.08	7,655,000.00	65.00	1,022.50
TULE LAKE	39,103.37	0.00	0.00	0.00	0.00	9.37	0.00	3.84	39,116.58
WILLOW CREEK-LURLINE	0.00	0.00	0.00	0.00	0.00	0.00	0.00	5,467.50	5,467.50
STATE TOTAL 38	79,823.09	67,454.86	35,325.49	6,117.84	9,687.99	149,645.07	186,181,154.06	122,542.15	470,596.49
COLORADO									
ALAMOSA	86.29	0.00	816.40	0.00	0.00	10,266.42	1,590,463.16	0.00	11,169.11
ARAPAHO	4,792.54	0.00	0.00	0.00	0.00	18,451.33	4,938,286.00	0.00	23,243.87
BROWNS PARK	6,794.30	0.00	0.00	0.00	0.00	5,355.53	642,976.00	1,305.47	13,455.30
COLORADO RIVER (45)*	0.00	0.00	17.64	0.00	0.00	0.00	0.00	161.31	178.95

TABLE 3 - NATIONAL WILDLIFE REFUGES

STATE AND UNIT	RESERVED FROM PUBLIC DOMAIN		ACQUIRED BY OTHER FEDERAL AGENCY		DEVISE OR GIFT	PURCHASED		AGREEMENT EASEMENT OR LEASE	TOTAL ACRES
	SOLE OR PRIMARY	SECONDARY	SOLE OR PRIMARY	SECONDARY		ACRES	COST ($)		
COLORADO									
FSA INTEREST CO ** *	0.00	0.00	0.00	0.00	0.00	0.00	0.00	296.00	296.00
MONTE VISTA	800.00	0.00	0.00	0.00	83.33	13,950.66	2,241,750.00	0.00	14,833.99
ROCKY MOUNTAIN ARSENAL	0.00	0.00	0.00	E 17,000.00	0.00	0.00	0.00	0.00	17,000.00
TWO PONDS	0.00	0.00	0.00	0.00	7.10	64.94	3,946,103.20	0.00	72.04
STATE TOTAL 6	12,473.13	0.00	834.04	17,000.00	90.43	48,088.88	13,359,578.36	1,762.78	80,249.26
CONNECTICUT									
STEWART B. MCKINNEY	0.00	0.00	0.00	CG 4.90	243.79	621.93	15,753,590.00	1.72	872.34
STATE TOTAL 1	0.00	0.00	0.00	4.90	243.79	621.93	15,753,590.00	1.72	872.34
DELAWARE									
BOMBAY HOOK	0.00	0.00	541.50	0.00	0.00	15,436.26	1,637,288.60	80.00	16,057.76
FSA INTEREST DE ** *	0.00	0.00	0.00	0.00	0.00	0.00	0.00	2.60	2.60
PRIME HOOK	0.00	0.00	0.00	0.00	29.60	9,165.90	6,219,464.16	870.59	10,066.09
STATE TOTAL 2	0.00	0.00	541.50	0.00	29.60	24,602.16	7,856,752.76	953.19	26,126.45
FLORIDA									
ARCHIE CARR	0.00	0.00	1.42	0.00	76.99	42.64	11,778,928.00	112.98	234.03
ARTHUR R. MARSHALL	0.00	0.00	0.00	0.00	0.00	2,549.77	118,511.97	143,237.60	145,787.37
CALOOSAHATCHEE	40.00	0.00	0.00	0.00	0.00	0.00	0.00	0.00	40.00
CEDAR KEYS	378.61	0.00	0.00	0.00	0.00	342.54	681,190.00	170.00	891.15
CHASSAHOWITZKA	320.56	0.00	0.00	0.00	0.00	30,522.35	496,746.12	0.00	30,842.91
CROCODILE LAKE	0.00	0.00	0.00	0.00	40.63	6,521.65	15,092,844.00	125.76	6,688.04
CRYSTAL RIVER	0.00	0.00	0.00	0.00	0.00	80.13	1,132,180.00	0.00	80.13
EGMONT KEY	328.30	0.00	0.00	0.00	0.00	0.00	0.00	0.00	328.30
FLORIDA PANTHER	0.00	0.00	0.00	0.00	594.00	25,935.04	10,232,916.68	0.00	26,529.04
FSA INTEREST FL ** *	0.00	0.00	241.74	0.00	0.00	0.00	0.00	2,881.79	3,123.53
GREAT WHITE HERON	770.40	0.00	264.95	0.00	288.24	5,181.99	5,158,327.77	186,287.05	192,787.63
HOBE SOUND	0.00	0.00	0.00	0.00	1,020.94	4.28	18,000.00	8.50	1,033.72
ISLAND BAY	20.24	0.00	0.00	0.00	0.00	0.00	0.00	0.00	20.24
J. N. DING DARLING	407.02	0.00	0.00	0.00	366.20	4,440.42	4,826,381.50	1,174.64	6,388.28
KEY WEST	1,865.17	CG 154.00	0.00	0.00	0.00	0.00	0.00	206,289.00	208,308.17
LAKE WALES RIDGE	0.00	0.00	0.00	0.00	0.00	1,840.40	3,291,600.00	0.00	1,840.40
LAKE WOODRUFF	0.00	0.00	7.00	0.00	642.66	18,502.36	1,404,690.75	2,407.00	21,559.02
LOWER SUWANNEE	0.00	0.00	0.00	0.00	75.00	49,124.38	13,652,060.00	1,831.14	51,030.52
MATLACHA PASS	277.61	0.00	0.00	0.00	115.03	0.00	0.00	0.00	392.64
MERRITT ISLAND	0.00	0.00	0.00	NA 138,262.70	0.00	925.70	1,335,689.00	1.00	139,189.40
NATIONAL KEY DEER	52.78	0.00	0.00	0.00	805.85	7,836.57	27,145,058.41	257.11	8,952.31
OKEFENOKEE (1)	0.00	0.00	0.00	0.00	0.00	3,678.14	52,636.00	46.34	3,724.48
PASSAGE KEY	36.37	0.00	0.00	0.00	0.00	0.00	0.00	27.50	63.87
PELICAN ISLAND	43.00	0.00	0.00	0.00	0.00	345.63	22,029,210.00	4,987.30	5,375.93
PINE ISLAND	175.17	0.00	0.00	0.00	0.00	427.07	2,434,000.00	0.00	602.24
PINELLAS	0.00	0.00	0.00	0.00	0.00	17.35	23,000.00	377.00	394.35
ST. JOHNS	0.00	0.00	0.00	0.00	2.50	6,254.95	2,878,323.64	0.00	6,257.45
ST. MARKS	93.20	0.00	31,709.49	0.00	363.64	35,054.45	1,743,811.61	402.29	67,623.07
ST. VINCENT	45.33	0.00	0.00	0.00	0.00	12,444.60	2,035,000.00	0.00	12,489.93
TEN THOUSAND ISLANDS	0.00	0.00	0.00	0.00	0.00	35,000.00	0.00	33.60	35,033.60
STATE TOTAL 29	4,853.76	154.00	32,224.60	138,262.70	4,586.68	247,072.41	125,561,105.45	550,657.60	977,611.75
GEORGIA									
BANKS LAKE	0.00	0.00	490.00	0.00	0.00	3,069.00	356,000.00	0.00	3,559.00
BLACKBEARD ISLAND	0.00	0.00	4,658.64	0.00	0.00	959.00	0.00	0.00	5,617.64
BOND SWAMP	0.00	0.00	0.00	0.00	0.00	5,490.25	2,758,250.00	0.00	5,490.25
EUFAULA (5) *	0.00	0.00	0.00	E 3,231.00	0.00	0.00	0.00	0.00	3,231.00
FSA INTEREST GA ** *	0.00	0.00	886.38	0.00	0.00	0.00	0.00	3,909.19	4,795.57

TABLE 3 - NATIONAL WILDLIFE REFUGES

STATE AND UNIT	RESERVED FROM PUBLIC DOMAIN		ACQUIRED BY OTHER FEDERAL AGENCY		DEVISE OR GIFT	PURCHASED		AGREEMENT EASEMENT OR LEASE	TOTAL ACRES
	SOLE OR PRIMARY	SECONDARY	SOLE OR PRIMARY	SECONDARY		ACRES	COST ($)		
GEORGIA									
HARRIS NECK	0.00	0.00	2,686.94	0.00	0.00	66.41	450,000.00	70.57	2,823.92
OKEFENOKEE (6) *	0.00	0.00	1,860.44	0.00	15,403.63	374,137.92	1,780,185.12	0.00	391,401.99
PIEDMONT	0.00	0.00	24,238.22	0.00	0.00	10,717.46	44,000.00	11.30	34,966.98
SAVANNAH (7)	0.00	0.00	4,015.04	0.00	0.00	9,280.17	3,321,852.40	28.27	13,323.48
WASSAW	0.00	0.00	0.00	0.00	10,049.87	0.00	0.00	20.00	10,069.87
WOLF ISLAND	0.00	0.00	538.00	0.00	0.00	4,587.82	120,813.52	0.00	5,125.82
STATE TOTAL 8	0.00	0.00	39,373.66	3,231.00	25,453.50	408,508.03	8,851,101.04	4,059.35	480,405.52
HAWAII									
HAKALAU FOREST	0.00	0.00	0.00	0.00	0.00	38,005.12	26,178,265.00	25.32	38,030.44
HANALEI	0.00	0.00	0.00	0.00	0.00	917.42	1,289,080.60	0.00	917.42
HAWAIIAN ISLANDS	254,418.10	0.00	0.00	0.00	0.00	0.00	0.00	0.00	254,418.10
HULEIA	0.00	0.00	0.00	0.00	0.00	240.17	327,623.00	.94	241.11
JAMES CAMPBELL	0.00	0.00	0.00	0.00	0.00	0.00	0.00	165.51	165.51
KAKAHAIA	0.00	0.00	0.00	0.00	0.00	44.61	684,550.00	0.00	44.61
KEALIA POND	0.00	0.00	0.00	0.00	0.00	0.00	0.00	691.56	691.56
KILAUEA POINT	0.00	0.00	31.00	0.00	91.38	59.48	6,475,000.00	16.82	198.68
OAHU FOREST	0.00	0.00	0.00	0.00	0.00	4,524.66	3,620,000.00	44.90	4,569.56
PEARL HARBOR	0.00	0.00	37.37	N 61.15	0.00	0.00	0.00	0.00	98.52
STATE TOTAL 10	254,418.10	0.00	68.37	61.15	91.38	43,791.46	38,574,518.60	945.05	299,375.51
IDAHO									
BEAR LAKE	16,977.61	0.00	0.00	0.00	0.00	1,107.97	339,879.30	0.00	18,085.58
CAMAS	0.00	0.00	0.00	0.00	0.00	10,578.34	202,700.84	0.00	10,578.34
DEER FLAT (4)	1,007.96	R 9,993.28	0.00	0.00	21.26	242.89	26,415.50	0.00	11,265.39
FSA INTEREST ID ** *	0.00	0.00	998.60	0.00	0.00	0.00	0.00	112.00	1,110.60
GRAYS LAKE	80.00	0.00	0.00	0.00	160.00	3,903.93	1,833,100.00	15,421.15	19,565.08
KOOTENAI	0.00	0.00	0.00	0.00	0.00	2,774.15	708,100.00	.14	2,774.29
MINIDOKA	2,863.93	R 16,764.87	0.00	R 1,070.32	0.00	0.00	0.00	2.49	20,701.61
STATE TOTAL 6	20,929.50	26,758.15	998.60	1,070.32	181.26	18,607.28	3,110,195.64	15,535.78	84,080.89
ILLINOIS									
CHAUTAUQUA	0.00	0.00	0.00	0.00	1,708.54	4,488.41	30,592.80	248.62	6,445.57
CRAB ORCHARD	0.00	0.00	42,507.58	0.00	0.00	1,380.94	436,103.50	0.00	43,888.52
CYPRESS CREEK	0.00	0.00	0.00	0.00	0.00	15,099.47	11,233,328.20	0.00	15,099.47
EMIQUON	0.00	0.00	0.00	0.00	0.00	2,154.94	3,145,400.00	0.00	2,154.94
FSA INTEREST IL ** *	0.00	0.00	335.40	0.00	0.00	0.00	0.00	0.00	335.40
GREAT RIVER (8)	0.00	0.00	0.00	E 5,490.81	59.95	1,559.87	353,202.72	0.00	7,110.63
MEREDOSIA	0.00	0.00	0.00	0.00	2,141.49	1,259.31	1,328,790.00	0.00	3,400.80
MIDDLE MISSISSIPPI RIVER (8)	0.00	0.00	0.00	0.00	0.00	2,237.53	399,795.00	0.00	2,237.53
PORT LOUISA (19)	0.00	0.00	0.00	E 1,466.00	0.00	4.60	11,500.00	.29	1,470.89
TWO RIVERS (8)	0.00	0.00	0.00	E 7,017.00	2.31	853.17	462,343.75	160.72	8,033.20
UPPER MISSISSIPPI RIVER (9)	65.15	0.00	322.66	E 20,120.00	0.00	· 2,924.73	48,619.97	.19	23,432.73
STATE TOTAL 10	65.15	0.00	43,165.64	34,093.81	3,912.29	31,962.97	17,449,675.94	409.82	113,609.68
INDIANA									
BIG OAKS	0.00	0.00	0.00	A 51,000.00	0.00	0.00	0.00	0.00	51,000.00
FSA INTEREST IN ** *	0.00	0.00	219.03	0.00	0.00	0.00	0.00	0.00	219.03
MUSCATATUCK	0.00	0.00	0.00	0.00	78.23	7,723.99	3,612,837.72	0.00	7,802.22
PATOKA RIVER	0.00	0.00	0.00	0.00	334.35	5,257.89	4,293,354.88	0.00	5,592.24
STATE TOTAL 3	0.00	0.00	219.03	51,000.00	412.58	12,981.88	7,906,192.60	0.00	64,613.49
IOWA									
DESOTO (10)	0.00	0.00	0.00	0.00	0.00	3,499.16	735,409.28	3.61	3,502.77
DRIFTLESS AREA	0.00	0.00	0.00	0.00	0.00	776.84	429,718.50	0.00	776.84

TABLE 3 - NATIONAL WILDLIFE REFUGES

STATE AND UNIT	RESERVED FROM PUBLIC DOMAIN		ACQUIRED BY OTHER FEDERAL AGENCY		DEVISE OR GIFT	PURCHASED		AGREEMENT EASEMENT OR LEASE	TOTAL ACRES
	SOLE OR PRIMARY	SECONDARY	SOLE OR PRIMARY	SECONDARY		ACRES	COST ($)		
IOWA									
NEAL SMITH	0.00	0.00	0.00	0.00	0.00	5,366.35	7,502,780.00	0.00	5,366.35
NORTHERN TALLGRASS PRAIRI (47)	0.00	0.00	0.00	0.00	0.00	160.00	176,000.00	0.00	160.00
PORT LOUISA (11)*	0.00	0.00	0.00	E 10,423.94	80.00	12,119.43	2,680,549.54	0.00	22,623.37
UNION SLOUGH	0.00	0.00	0.00	0.00	0.00	2,845.24	210,407.69	70.70	2,915.94
UPPER MISSISSIPPI RIVER (13)*	333.66	0.00	0.00	E 30,315.00	.57	20,389.98	409,867.96	0.00	51,039.21
STATE TOTAL 5	333.66	0.00	0.00	40,738.94	80.57	45,157.00	12,144,752.97	74.31	86,384.48
KANSAS									
FLINT HILLS	0.00	0.00	0.00	E 18,463.21	0.00	0.00	0.00	.15	18,463.36
FSA INTEREST KS ** *	0.00	0.00	116.50	0.00	0.00	0.00	0.00	0.00	116.50
KIRWIN	0.00	0.00	0.00	R 10,778.00	0.00	0.00	0.00	0.00	10,778.00
MARAIS DES CYGNES	0.00	0.00	0.00	0.00	0.00	7,303.34	3,113,761.40	0.00	7,303.34
QUIVIRA	0.00	0.00	0.00	0.00	199.20	21,820.10	2,059,258.00	0.00	22,019.30
STATE TOTAL 4	0.00	0.00	116.50	29,241.21	199.20	29,123.44	5,173,019.40	.15	58,680.50
KENTUCKY									
CLARKS RIVER	0.00	0.00	0.00	0.00	0.00	6,613.61	5,818,751.00	0.00	6,613.61
OHIO RIVER ISLANDS (38)*	0.00	0.00	0.00	0.00	0.00	404.56	288,640.00	0.00	404.56
REELFOOT (14)	0.00	0.00	0.00	0.00	0.00	2,039.64	418,450.15	0.00	2,039.64
STATE TOTAL 2	0.00	0.00	0.00	0.00	0.00	9,057.81	6,525,841.15	0.00	9,057.81
LOUISIANA									
ATCHAFALAYA	0.00	0.00	0.00	0.00	0.00	15,255.25	11,065,618.00	0.00	15,255.25
BAYOU COCODRIE	0.00	0.00	0.00	0.00	0.00	13,168.51	7,016,578.00	0.00	13,168.51
BAYOU SAUVAGE	0.00	0.00	0.00	0.00	0.00	22,263.05	10,959,000.00	0.00	22,263.05
BAYOU TECHE	0.00	0.00	0.00	0.00	0.00	9,073.50	2,254,000.00	0.00	9,073.50
BIG BRANCH MARSH	0.00	0.00	0.00	0.00	11,586.54	4,417.25	8,514,174.00	0.00	16,003.79
BLACK BAYOU LAKE	0.00	0.00	0.00	0.00	0.00	2,272.01	5,033,500.00	1,620.00	3,892.01
BOGUE CHITTO (27)	0.00	0.00	0.00	0.00	35.00	28,755.79	13,458,223.85	762.00	29,552.79
BRETON	9,047.00	0.00	0.00	0.00	0.00	0.00	0.00	0.00	9,047.00
CAMERON PRAIRIE	0.00	0.00	0.00	0.00	0.00	9,621.30	5,090,650.00	0.00	9,621.30
CAT ISLAND	0.00	0.00	0.00	0.00	13.40	2,341.51	2,312,779.00	0.00	2,354.91
CATAHOULA	0.00	0.00	0.00	0.00	0.00	14,909.61	2,191,497.25	0.00	14,909.61
D'ARBONNE	0.00	0.00	17,419.63	0.00	0.00	0.00	0.00	0.00	17,419.63
DELTA	1,407.65	E 2,892.30	10,036.42	0.00	0.00	34,462.73	233,324.17	0.00	48,799.10
FSA INTEREST LA ** *	0.00	0.00	8,445.51	0.00	0.00	0.00	0.00	5,580.44	14,025.95
GRAND COTE	0.00	0.00	0.00	0.00	0.00	5,997.00	1,776,000.00	80.00	6,077.00
HANDY BRAKE	0.00	0.00	465.70	0.00	0.00	0.00	0.00	35.00	500.70
LACASSINE	0.00	0.00	22,991.51	0.00	0.00	10,734.75	1,558,256.43	652.51	34,378.77
LAKE OPHELIA	0.00	0.00	13.70	0.00	0.00	17,341.46	7,370,080.00	200.00	17,555.16
MANDALAY	0.00	0.00	0.00	0.00	4,416.00	0.00	0.00	203.00	4,619.00
RED RIVER	0.00	0.00	0.00	0.00	0.00	1,377.14	1,000,000.00	2,480.00	3,857.14
SABINE	0.00	0.00	138,870.15	0.00	0.00	566.66	14,000.51	1,280.00	140,716.81
SHELL KEYS	8.00	0.00	0.00	0.00	0.00	0.00	0.00	0.00	8.00
TENSAS RIVER	0.00	0.00	53,174.58	0.00	526.85	12,498.57	9,356,010.00	195.17	66,395.17
UPPER OUACHITA	0.00	0.00	0.00	0.00	0.00	42,594.98	20,596,936.00	3,265.83	45,860.81
STATE TOTAL 23	10,462.65	2,892.30	251,417.20	0.00	16,577.79	247,651.05	109,760,627.21	16,353.95	545,354.94
MAINE									
AROOSTOOK	0.00	0.00	4,458.50	0.00	0.00	196.57	62,120.00	0.00	4,655.07
CROSS ISLAND	0.00	0.00	0.00	0.00	1,538.40	164.70	0.00	0.00	1,703.10
FRANKLIN ISLAND	0.00	0.00	11.94	0.00	0.00	0.00	0.00	0.00	11.94
FSA INTEREST ME ** *	0.00	0.00	394.08	0.00	0.00	0.00	0.00	228.00	622.08
LAKE UMBAGOG (36)*	0.00	0.00	0.00	0.00	24.32	4,341.55	3,736,420.00	0.00	4,365.87
MOOSEHORN	0.00	0.00	6,490.33	0.00	332.64	20,776.96	5,032,399.19	80.32	27,680.45

TABLE 3 - NATIONAL WILDLIFE REFUGES

STATE AND UNIT	RESERVED FROM PUBLIC DOMAIN		ACQUIRED BY OTHER FEDERAL AGENCY		DEVISE OR GIFT	PURCHASED		AGREEMENT EASEMENT OR LEASE	TOTAL ACRES
	SOLE OR PRIMARY	SECONDARY	SOLE OR PRIMARY	SECONDARY		ACRES	COST ($)		
MAINE									
PETIT MANAN	0.00	0.00	106.42	0.00	1,650.02	3,625.46	5,005,445.00	274.96	5,656.86
POND ISLAND	0.00	0.00	10.00	0.00	0.00	0.00	0.00	0.00	10.00
RACHEL CARSON	0.00	0.00	0.00	0.00	581.11	4,356.03	14,782,906.75	150.54	5,087.68
SEAL ISLAND	0.00	0.00	65.00	0.00	0.00	0.00	0.00	0.00	65.00
SUNKHAZE MEADOWS	0.00	0.00	0.00	0.00	126.30	10,064.00	2,249,950.00	0.00	10,190.30
STATE TOTAL 9	0.00	0.00	11,556.27	0.00	4,252.99	43,525.27	30,869,240.94	753.82	60,048.35
MARYLAND									
BLACKWATER	0.00	0.00	0.00	0.00	1,370.73	23,619.14	11,831,764.01	0.00	24,989.87
CHINCOTEAGUE (16)*	0.00	0.00	0.00	0.00	0.00	417.81	13,780.42	0.00	417.81
EASTERN NECK	0.00	0.00	0.00	0.00	0.00	2,286.27	1,606,145.09	0.00	2,286.27
FSA INTEREST MD ** *	0.00	0.00	0.00	0.00	0.00	0.00	0.00	67.94	67.94
MARTIN (16)	0.00	0.00	0.00	0.00	2,569.86	1,853.57	61,027.00	0.00	4,423.43
PATUXENT	0.00	0.00	11,852.10	0.00	0.00	988.83	1,310,786.71	.27	12,841.20
SUSQUEHANNA	0.00	0.00	3.79	0.00	0.00	0.00	0.00	0.00	3.79
STATE TOTAL 5	0.00	0.00	11,855.89	0.00	3,940.59	29,165.62	14,823,503.23	68.21	45,030.31
MASSACHUSETTS									
ASSABET RIVER	0.00	0.00	2,229.20	0.00	0.00	0.00	0.00	0.00	2,229.20
GREAT MEADOWS	0.00	0.00	0.00	0.00	284.53	3,399.73	8,909,500.90	27.33	3,711.59
MASHPEE	0.00	0.00	0.00	0.00	3.00	284.40	2,810,000.00	54.25	341.65
MASSASOIT	0.00	0.00	0.00	0.00	0.00	198.11	605,432.00	0.00	198.11
MONOMOY	0.00	0.00	2.10	0.00	0.00	2,699.75	149,465.00	0.00	2,701.85
NANTUCKET	0.00	0.00	24.00	0.00	0.00	0.00	0.00	0.00	24.00
NOMANS LAND ISLAND	0.00	0.00	628.00	0.00	0.00	0.00	0.00	0.00	628.00
OXBOW	0.00	0.00	1,547.33	0.00	4.29	125.40	3,410,000.00	0.00	1,677.02
PARKER RIVER	0.00	0.00	1.90	0.00	0.00	4,650.61	537,740.84	0.00	4,652.51
SILVIO O. CONTE (42)*	0.00	0.00	0.00	0.00	3.80	181.89	1,398,210.00	0.00	185.69
THACHER ISLAND	0.00	0.00	22.00	0.00	0.00	0.00	0.00	0.00	22.00
STATE TOTAL 10	0.00	0.00	4,454.53	0.00	295.62	11,539.89	17,820,348.74	81.58	16,371.62
MICHIGAN									
DETROIT RIVER	304.47	0.00	0.00	0.00	21.15	0.00	0.00	0.00	325.62
FSA INTEREST MI ** *	0.00	0.00	94.00	0.00	0.00	0.00	0.00	0.00	94.00
HARBOR ISLAND	0.00	0.00	0.00	0.00	0.00	695.00	197,000.00	0.00	695.00
HURON	22.50	0.00	124.35	0.00	0.00	0.00	0.00	0.00	146.85
KIRTLANDS WARBLER	0.00	0.00	0.00	0.00	0.00	6,684.46	3,526,886.40	0.00	6,684.46
MICHIGAN ISLANDS	11.94 CG	121.70	229.70	0.00	234.05	0.00	0.00	0.00	597.39
SENEY	2,660.60	0.00	7,058.59	0.00	0.00	86,525.62	177,178.95	0.00	95,244.81
SHIAWASSEE	0.00	0.00	0.00	0.00	52.21	8,960.54	2,470,375.67	350.00	9,362.75
STATE TOTAL 7	2,999.51	121.70	7,506.64	0.00	307.41	101,865.62	6,371,441.02	350.00	113,150.88
MINNESOTA									
AGASSIZ	6.00	0.00	60,091.88	0.00	0.00	954.30	40,226.04	448.75	61,500.93
BIG STONE	0.00	0.00	10,540.43 E	254.20	0.00	725.50	639,200.00	0.00	11,520.13
CRANE MEADOWS	0.00	0.00	0.00	0.00	20.00	1,667.50	1,155,965.00	0.00	1,687.50
FSA INTEREST MN ** *	0.00	0.00	1,783.80	0.00	0.00	0.00	0.00	0.00	1,783.80
HAMDEN SLOUGH	0.00	0.00	0.00	0.00	0.00	3,120.45	1,787,872.00	73.40	3,193.85
MILLE LACS	.60	0.00	0.00	0.00	0.00	0.00	0.00	0.00	.60
MINNESOTA VALLEY	0.00	0.00	364.98	0.00	1,268.51	7,347.20	19,912,153.63	1,703.44	10,684.13
NORTHERN TALLGRASS PRAIRI (19)*	0.00	0.00	0.00	0.00	0.00	353.40	150,195.00	306.31	659.71
RICE LAKE	0.00	0.00	9,831.57	0.00	0.00	6,640.71	265,329.77	0.00	16,472.28
RYDELL	0.00	0.00	0.00	0.00	2,070.00	0.00	0.00	0.00	2,070.00
SHERBURNE	0.00	0.00	0.00	0.00	0.00	29,607.44	3,273,341.05	0.00	29,607.44
TAMARAC	40.00	0.00	0.00	0.00	0.00	35,151.38	612,159.93	0.00	35,191.38

TABLE 3 - NATIONAL WILDLIFE REFUGES

STATE AND UNIT	RESERVED FROM PUBLIC DOMAIN		ACQUIRED BY OTHER FEDERAL AGENCY		DEVISE OR GIFT	PURCHASED		AGREEMENT EASEMENT OR LEASE	TOTAL ACRES
	SOLE OR PRIMARY	SECONDARY	SOLE OR PRIMARY	SECONDARY		ACRES	COST ($)		
MINNESOTA									
UPPER MISSISSIPPI RIVER (18)*	241.58	0.00	0.00	E 15,420.77	140.92	17,772.56	385,404.80	92.97	33,668.80
STATE TOTAL 10	288.18	0.00	82,612.66	15,674.97	3,499.43	103,340.44	28,221,847.22	2,624.87	208,040.55
MISSISSIPPI									
BOGUE CHITTO (28)*	0.00	0.00	0.00	0.00	0.00	6,949.08	6,695,784.00	0.00	6,949.08
COLDWATER RIVER	0.00	0.00	94.26	0.00	0.00	2,374.10	1,430,450.00	0.00	2,468.36
DAHOMEY	0.00	0.00	0.00	0.00	162.00	8,744.80	4,900,000.00	260.00	9,166.80
FSA INTEREST MS ** *	0.00	0.00	21,755.38	0.00	0.00	0.00	0.00	6,940.71	28,696.09
GRAND BAY (5) *	0.00	0.00	0.00	0.00	4,456.63	2,656.53	2,228,383.00	0.00	7,113.16
HILLSIDE	0.00	0.00	15,383.13	0.00	22.74	3,645.52	2,879,100.00	0.00	19,051.39
MATHEWS BRAKE	0.00	0.00	0.00	0.00	0.00	2,418.74	1,691,446.00	0.00	2,418.74
MISSISSIPPI SANDHILL CRANE	0.00	0.00	0.00	0.00	20.15	18,016.50	21,115,501.00	1,679.28	19,715.93
MORGAN BRAKE	0.00	0.00	0.00	0.00	131.84	7,241.28	4,517,482.20	0.00	7,373.11
NOXUBEE	40.08	0.00	35,343.85	0.00	80.00	11,585.26	145,413.05	0.00	47,049.19
PANTHER SWAMP	0.00	0.00	0.00	E 7,070.45	0.00	27,559.89	15,015,723.00	641.51	35,271.85
ST. CATHERINE CREEK	0.00	0.00	0.00	0.00	0.00	24,429.29	12,925,167.00	502.10	24,931.39
TALLAHATCHIE	0.00	0.00	0.00	0.00	0.00	2,207.00	1,171,000.00	470.00	2,677.00
YAZOO	0.00	0.00	0.00	0.00	0.00	13,022.98	2,760,803.78	0.00	13,022.98
STATE TOTAL 11	40.08	0.00	72,576.62	7,070.45	4,873.35	130,850.97	77,476,253.03	10,493.60	225,905.07
MISSOURI									
BIG MUDDY	0.00	0.00	442.00	A 1,300.00	0.00	6,403.21	2,267,405.00	1.68	8,146.89
CLARENCE CANNON	0.00	0.00	0.00	0.00	0.00	3,749.98	1,175,364.25	0.00	3,749.98
FSA INTEREST MO ** *	0.00	0.00	1,673.06	0.00	0.00	0.00	0.00	111.62	1,784.68
GREAT RIVER (11)*	0.00	0.00	0.00	0.00	0.00	2,107.93	999,500.00	0.00	2,107.93
MIDDLE MISSISSIPPI RIVER (11)*	0.00	0.00	0.00	0.00	0.00	1,704.17	1,914,805.00	0.00	1,704.17
MINGO	0.00	0.00	0.00	0.00	0.00	21,676.06	317,365.62	69.80	21,745.86
OZARK CAVEFISH	0.00	0.00	0.00	0.00	0.00	41.80	152,000.00	0.00	41.80
PILOT KNOB	0.00	0.00	0.00	0.00	90.00	0.00	0.00	0.00	90.00
SQUAW CREEK	0.00	0.00	3,049.10	0.00	0.00	4,300.96	573,149.19	64.83	7,414.89
SWAN LAKE	0.00	0.00	5,923.42	0.00	0.00	5,569.55	355,194.19	0.00	11,492.97
TWO RIVERS (11)*	0.00	0.00	0.00	E 232.00	0.00	0.00	0.00	0.00	232.00
STATE TOTAL 7	0.00	0.00	11,087.58	1,532.00	90.00	45,553.66	7,754,781.45	247.93	58,511.17
MONTANA									
BENTON LAKE	12,234.92	0.00	0.00	0.00	0.00	147.64	5,315.00	76.88	12,459.44
BLACK COULEE	640.00	0.00	0.00	0.00	0.00	0.00	0.00	668.88	1,308.88
BLACKFOOT VALLEY	0.00	0.00	0.00	0.00	0.00	0.00	0.00	8,164.36	8,164.36
BOWDOIN	14,796.58	0.00	640.00	0.00	0.00	0.00	0.00	115.39	15,551.97
CHARLES M. RUSSELL	358,196.42	E 380,901.03	8,574.02	E 147,399.11	55.37	10,875.87	2,626,780.00	6,346.50	912,348.32
CREEDMAN COULEE	80.00	0.00	0.00	0.00	0.00	0.00	0.00	2,648.00	2,728.00
FSA INTEREST MT ** *	0.00	0.00	270.62	0.00	0.00	0.00	0.00	240.00	510.62
HAILSTONE	0.00	GS 160.00	0.00	0.00	0.00	0.00	0.00	760.00	920.00
HALFBREED LAKE	0.00	0.00	0.00	0.00	0.00	3,279.02	291,000.00	1,039.22	4,318.24
HEWITT LAKE	0.00	GS 400.00	320.49	0.00	0.00	0.00	0.00	640.43	1,360.92
LAKE MASON	17.59	0.00	6,981.65	0.00	0.00	4,256.60	18,500.00	5,558.68	16,814.52
LAKE THIBADEAU	19.42	0.00	0.00	0.00	0.00	0.00	0.00	3,849.06	3,868.48
LAMESTEER	0.00	0.00	0.00	0.00	0.00	0.00	0.00	800.00	800.00
LEE METCALF	0.00	0.00	0.00	0.00	0.00	2,792.52	868,080.00	0.00	2,792.52
LOST TRAIL	0.00	0.00	0.00	0.00	3,112.00	4,693.20	1,728,205.00	1,029.04	8,834.24
MEDICINE LAKE	1,520.99	0.00	27,419.81	0.00	3.64	2,513.26	25,460.00	26.31	31,484.01
NATIONAL BISON RANGE	0.00	0.00	18,479.50	0.00	0.00	320.34	477,200.00	0.00	18,799.84
NINE-PIPE	0.00	0.00	0.00	0.00	0.00	0.00	0.00	4,027.68	4,027.68
PABLO	0.00	0.00	0.00	0.00	0.00	0.00	0.00	2,541.95	2,541.95

TABLE 3 - NATIONAL WILDLIFE REFUGES

STATE AND UNIT	RESERVED FROM PUBLIC DOMAIN		ACQUIRED BY OTHER FEDERAL AGENCY		DEVISE OR GIFT	PURCHASED		AGREEMENT EASEMENT OR LEASE	TOTAL ACRES
	SOLE OR PRIMARY	SECONDARY	SOLE OR PRIMARY	SECONDARY		ACRES	COST ($)		
MONTANA									
RED ROCK LAKES	9,218.31 F	594.28	29,485.58	0.00	340.00	5,961.54	2,658,869.00	6,146.70	51,744.41
SWAN RIVER	0.00	0.00	0.00	0.00	0.00	1,568.81	901,645.00	0.00	1,568.81
UL BEND	29,678.22 E	6,897.46	1,299.79 E	7,925.90	0.00	9,688.19	577,280.00	560.00	56,049.56
WAR HORSE	0.00	0.00	3,192.24	0.00	0.00	0.00	0.00	0.00	3,192.24
STATE TOTAL 22	426,402.45	388,952.77	96,661.70	155,325.01	3,511.01	46,096.99	10,178,324.00	45,239.08	1,162,189.01
NEBRASKA									
BOYER CHUTE	0.00	0.00	0.00	0.00	1,953.85	1,346.42	3,486,960.92	0.00	3,300.27
CRESCENT LAKE	265.87	0.00	240.00	0.00	0.00	45,457.99	323,115.00	31.49	45,995.35
DESOTO (19)*	0.00	0.00	0.00	0.00	0.00	4,324.20	761,275.20	0.00	4,324.20
FORT NIOBRARA	14,778.12	0.00	2,383.91	0.00	8.05	1,962.45	34,309.32	0.00	19,132.53
FSA INTEREST NE ** *	0.00	0.00	683.70	0.00	0.00	0.00	0.00	1,409.02	2,092.72
JOHN W. & LOUISE SEIER	0.00	0.00	0.00	0.00	2,400.00	0.00	0.00	0.00	2,400.00
KARL E. MUNDT (20)*	0.00	0.00	0.00	0.00	19.39	0.00	0.00	0.00	19.39
NORTH PLATTE	742.89 R	2,684.81	0.00	0.00	0.00	45.53	27,500.00	0.00	3,473.23
VALENTINE	0.00	0.00	65,114.00	0.00	0.00	6,599.84	78,572.00	1,324.25	73,038.09
STATE TOTAL 6	15,786.88	2,684.81	68,421.61	0.00	4,381.29	59,736.43	4,711,752.44	2,764.76	153,775.78
NEVADA									
ANAHO ISLAND	247.73	0.00	0.00	0.00	0.00	0.00	0.00	0.00	247.73
ASH MEADOWS	0.00	0.00	0.00	0.00	0.00	13,359.34	6,462,600.00	382.00	13,741.34
DESERT	1,588,055.10	0.00	0.00	0.00	3.45	760.00	592,800.00	0.00	1,588,818.55
FALLON	0.00 R	17,901.94	0.00	0.00	0.00	0.00	0.00	0.00	17,901.94
MOAPA VALLEY	0.00	0.00	0.00	0.00	0.00	104.26	2,080,000.00	0.00	104.26
PAHRANAGAT	1,466.39	0.00	0.00	0.00	0.00	3,915.60	500,000.00	.75	5,382.74
RUBY LAKE	7,565.53 LM	120.00	0.00	0.00	0.00	31,600.57	208,457.25	0.00	39,286.10
SHELDON (4)	544,276.82 LM	80.00	0.00	0.00	2,535.66	25,983.67	582,502.00	0.00	572,876.15
STILLWATER	76,799.00	0.00	0.00	0.00	0.00	10,069.53	12,557,539.00	26.41	86,894.94
STATE TOTAL 9	2,218,410.57	18,101.94	0.00	0.00	2,539.11	85,792.97	22,963,878.25	409.16	2,525,253.75
NEW HAMPSHIRE									
GREAT BAY	0.00	0.00	1,054.00	0.00	0.00	0.00	0.00	28.90	1,082.90
JOHN HAY	0.00	0.00	0.00	0.00	164.60	0.00	0.00	.30	164.90
LAKE UMBAGOG (37)	0.00	0.00	0.00	0.00	0.00	12,177.96	9,840,871.00	6.01	12,183.97
SILVIO O. CONTE (43)*	0.00	0.00	0.00	0.00	0.00	670.82	354,192.56	0.00	670.82
WAPACK	0.00	0.00	0.00	0.00	1,672.00	0.00	0.00	0.00	1,672.00
STATE TOTAL 4	0.00	0.00	1,054.00	0.00	1,836.60	12,848.78	10,195,063.96	35.21	15,774.59
NEW JERSEY									
CAPE MAY	0.00	0.00	0.00	0.00	0.00	10,419.58	24,116,335.22	490.80	10,910.38
EDWIN B. FORSYTHE	0.00	0.00	0.00	0.00	1,153.59	41,624.51	42,586,501.83	2,413.03	45,191.13
GREAT SWAMP	0.00	0.00	0.00	0.00	2,872.20	4,657.23	16,228,308.05	1.52	7,530.95
SUPAWNA MEADOWS	0.00	0.00	6.86	1.96 C	0.00	2,885.93	1,297,644.00	0.00	2,894.75
WALLKILL RIVER (39)*	0.00	0.00	0.00	0.00	0.00	4,669.61	19,986,355.00	0.00	4,669.61
STATE TOTAL 4	0.00	0.00	6.86	1.96	4,025.79	64,256.86	104,214,144.10	2,905.35	71,196.82
NEW MEXICO									
BITTER LAKE	12,395.71	0.00	0.00	0.00	0.00	12,212.93	843,804.00	0.00	24,608.64
BOSQUE DEL APACHE	140.00	0.00	0.00	0.00	0.00	56,850.31	125,311.00	200.79	57,191.10
GRULLA (12)	3,230.55	0.00	0.00	0.00	0.00	0.00	0.00	0.00	3,230.55
LAS VEGAS	0.00	0.00	0.00	0.00	0.00	8,672.08	2,121,150.00	0.00	8,672.08
MAXWELL	0.00	0.00	0.00	438.52 R	0.00	2,791.69	423,370.79	468.38	3,698.59
SAN ANDRES	0.00 LM	57,215.48	0.00	0.00	0.00	0.00	0.00	0.00	57,215.48
SEVILLETA	0.00	0.00	0.00	0.00	220,200.00	9,411.07	1,545,765.00	62.50	229,673.57
STATE TOTAL 7	15,766.26	57,215.48	0.00	438.52	220,200.00	89,938.08	5,059,400.79	731.67	384,290.01

TABLE 3 - NATIONAL WILDLIFE REFUGES

| STATE AND UNIT | RESERVED FROM PUBLIC DOMAIN | | ACQUIRED BY OTHER FEDERAL AGENCY | | DEVISE OR GIFT | PURCHASED | | AGREEMENT EASEMENT OR LEASE | TOTAL ACRES |
	SOLE OR PRIMARY	SECONDARY	SOLE OR PRIMARY	SECONDARY		ACRES	COST ($)		
NEW YORK									
AMAGANSETT	0.00	0.00	35.84	0.00	0.00	0.00	0.00	0.00	35.84
CONSCIENCE POINT	0.00	0.00	0.00	0.00	60.40	0.00	0.00	0.00	60.40
ELIZABETH A. MORTON	0.00	0.00	0.00	0.00	187.19	0.00	0.00	0.00	187.19
FSA INTEREST NY ** *	0.00	0.00	1,178.45	0.00	0.00	0.00	0.00	1,535.65	2,714.10
IROQUOIS	0.00	0.00	0.00	0.00	0.00	10,824.61	1,281,819.86	3.45	10,828.06
MONTEZUMA	0.00	0.00	0.00	0.00	12.31	8,036.88	2,449,050.01	407.85	8,457.04
OYSTER BAY	0.00	0.00	0.00	0.00	3,204.08	0.00	0.00	0.00	3,204.08
SEATUCK	0.00	0.00	0.00	0.00	209.23	0.00	0.00	0.00	209.23
SHAWANGUNK GRASSLANDS	0.00	0.00	566.53	0.00	0.00	0.00	0.00	0.00	566.53
TARGET ROCK	0.00	0.00	0.00	0.00	80.09	0.00	0.00	0.00	80.09
WALLKILL RIVER (40)	0.00	0.00	0.00	0.00	0.00	147.09	236,960.00	0.00	147.09
WERTHEIM	0.00	0.00	25.95	0.00	1,870.74	672.67	6,377,489.80	0.00	2,569.36
STATE TOTAL 11	0.00	0.00	1,806.77	0.00	5,624.04	19,681.25	10,345,319.67	1,946.95	29,059.01
NORTH CAROLINA									
ALLIGATOR RIVER	0.00	0.00	0.00	0.00	125,359.00	26,836.37	5,657,267.00	0.00	152,195.37
CEDAR ISLAND	0.00	0.00	31.40	0.00	1,966.15	12,484.77	347,171.21	0.00	14,482.32
CURRITUCK	0.00	0.00	0.00	0.00	0.00	4,098.88	6,696,048.00	3,930.76	8,029.64
FSA INTEREST NC ** *	0.00	0.00	565.49	0.00	0.00	0.00	0.00	5,868.55	6,434.04
GREAT DISMAL SWAMP (16)	0.00	0.00	0.00	0.00	10,957.00	15,152.70	5,682,554.47	0.00	26,109.70
MACKAY ISLAND (16)	0.00	0.00	0.00	0.00	841.88	6,421.46	1,046,906.95	.00	7,263.34
MATTAMUSKEET	0.00	0.00	49,925.05	0.00	0.00	252.04	1,285.35	3.09	50,180.18
PEA ISLAND	0.00	0.00	34.85	OG 11.38	0.00	5,787.97	40,401.86	0.00	5,834.20
PEE DEE	0.00	0.00	0.00	0.00	0.00	8,438.94	2,561,851.76	0.00	8,438.94
POCOSIN LAKES	0.00	0.00	0.00	0.00	97,718.29	12,350.35	1,682,157.99	37.90	110,106.54
ROANOKE RIVER	0.00	0.00	0.00	0.00	0.00	17,976.63	9,015,258.00	0.00	17,976.63
SWANQUARTER	0.00	0.00	0.00	0.00	910.33	15,500.76	61,000.93	0.00	16,411.09
STATE TOTAL 11	0.00	0.00	50,556.79	11.38	237,752.65	125,300.87	32,791,903.52	9,840.30	423,461.99
NORTH DAKOTA									
APPERT LAKE	0.00	0.00	0.00	0.00	0.00	0.00	0.00	907.75	907.75
ARDOCH	0.00	0.00	0.00	0.00	14.22	293.41	4,741.00	2,388.50	2,696.13
ARROWWOOD	4.28	0.00	11,248.72	0.00	3.34	2,097.51	46,906.58	2,589.01	15,942.86
AUDUBON	0.00	0.00	0.00	E 14,739.19	0.00	0.00	0.00	0.00	14,739.19
BONE HILL	0.00	0.00	0.00	0.00	0.00	0.00	0.00	640.00	640.00
BRUMBA	0.00	0.00	0.00	0.00	0.00	0.00	0.00	1,977.48	1,977.48
BUFFALO LAKE	23.80	0.00	0.00	0.00	0.00	0.00	0.00	1,539.92	1,563.72
CAMP LAKE	0.00	0.00	0.00	0.00	0.00	0.00	0.00	584.70	584.70
CANFIELD LAKE	0.00	0.00	0.00	0.00	0.00	3.10	100.00	310.13	313.23
CHASE LAKE	0.00	0.00	0.00	0.00	0.00	4,449.47	25,611.00	0.00	4,449.47
COTTONWOOD LAKE	0.00	0.00	0.00	0.00	0.00	0.00	0.00	1,013.47	1,013.47
DAKOTA LAKE	0.00	0.00	0.00	0.00	0.00	0.00	0.00	2,799.78	2,799.78
DAKOTA TALLGRASS PRAIRIE (20)	0.00	0.00	0.00	0.00	0.00	0.00	0.00	1,903.94	1,903.94
DES LACS	100.23	0.00	13,237.02	0.00	30.00	701.82	6,893.60	5,478.07	19,547.14
FLORENCE LAKE	0.00	0.00	0.00	0.00	0.00	1,468.40	31,485.00	419.80	1,888.20
FSA INTEREST ND ** *	0.00	0.00	0.00	0.00	0.00	0.00	0.00	6,591.40	6,591.40
HALF-WAY LAKE	0.00	0.00	0.00	0.00	0.00	0.00	0.00	160.00	160.00
HIDDENWOOD	0.00	0.00	0.00	0.00	0.00	0.00	0.00	568.35	568.35
HOBART LAKE	9.40	0.00	0.00	0.00	0.00	236.49	5,165.00	1,831.21	2,077.10
HUTCHINSON LAKE	0.00	0.00	0.00	0.00	0.00	0.00	0.00	478.90	478.90
J. CLARK SALYER	320.66	0.00	36,702.29	0.00	2.59	21,659.05	308,852.60	690.52	59,375.11
JOHNSON LAKE	0.00	0.00	0.00	0.00	4.49	0.00	0.00	2,003.42	2,007.91
KELLYS SLOUGH	680.00	0.00	0.00	0.00	0.00	0.00	0.00	589.50	1,269.50
LAKE ALICE	0.00	0.00	160.00	0.00	2.18	8,349.86	2,195,534.00	3,583.50	12,095.54

TABLE 3 - NATIONAL WILDLIFE REFUGES

STATE AND UNIT	RESERVED FROM PUBLIC DOMAIN		ACQUIRED BY OTHER FEDERAL AGENCY		DEVISE OR GIFT	PURCHASED		AGREEMENT EASEMENT OR LEASE	TOTAL ACRES
	SOLE OR PRIMARY	SECONDARY	SOLE OR PRIMARY	SECONDARY		ACRES	COST ($)		
NORTH DAKOTA LAKE GEORGE	29.20	0.00	0.00	0.00	0.00	0.00	0.00	3,089.61	3,118.81
LAKE ILO	0.00	0.00	0.00	0.00	10.71	3,186.50	116,422.98	835.91	4,033.12
LAKE NETTIE	0.00	0.00	0.00	0.00	0.00	2,420.60	148,245.00	634.30	3,054.90
LAKE OTIS	0.00	0.00	0.00	0.00	0.00	0.00	0.00	320.00	320.00
LAKE PATRICIA	0.00	0.00	0.00	0.00	0.00	0.00	0.00	800.23	800.23
LAKE ZAHL	40.00	0.00	0.00	0.00	0.00	3,178.98	53,275.00	604.21	3,823.19
LAMBS LAKE	0.00	0.00	0.00	0.00	0.00	0.00	0.00	1,206.67	1,206.67
LITTLE GOOSE	0.00	0.00	0.00	0.00	0.00	0.00	0.00	288.41	288.41
LONG LAKE	1,170.34	0.00	0.00	0.00	0.00	12,738.82	107,180.00	8,589.34	22,498.50
LORDS LAKE	0.00	0.00	0.00	0.00	0.00	0.00	0.00	1,915.29	1,915.29
LOST LAKE	0.00	0.00	0.00	0.00	0.00	0.00	0.00	960.21	960.21
LOSTWOOD	203.60	0.00	23,395.86	0.00	0.00	3,304.53	73,553.00	0.00	26,903.99
MAPLE RIVER	0.00	0.00	0.00	0.00	0.00	0.00	0.00	712.00	712.00
MCLEAN	0.00	0.00	0.00	0.00	0.00	344.00	12,516.00	416.00	760.00
NORTH DAKOTA	0.00	0.00	0.00	0.00	0.00	0.00	0.00	32,839.09	32,839.09
PLEASANT LAKE	0.00	0.00	0.00	0.00	0.00	0.00	0.00	897.80	897.80
PRETTY ROCK	0.00	0.00	0.00	0.00	0.00	0.00	0.00	800.00	800.00
RABB LAKE	0.00	0.00	0.00	0.00	0.00	0.00	0.00	260.80	260.80
ROCK LAKE	0.00	0.00	0.00	0.00	0.00	0.00	0.00	5,505.96	5,505.96
ROSE LAKE	0.00	0.00	0.00	0.00	0.00	0.00	0.00	836.30	836.30
SCHOOL SECTION LAKE	0.00	0.00	0.00	0.00	0.00	0.00	0.00	297.30	297.30
SHELL LAKE	0.00	0.00	0.00	0.00	0.00	785.20	38,902.00	1,124.90	1,910.10
SHEYENNE LAKE	0.00	0.00	0.00	0.00	0.00	0.00	0.00	797.30	797.30
SIBLEY LAKE	0.00	0.00	0.00	0.00	0.00	0.00	0.00	1,077.40	1,077.40
SILVER LAKE	0.00	0.00	0.00	0.00	0.00	0.00	0.00	3,347.64	3,347.64
SLADE	0.00	0.00	0.00	0.00	3,000.20	0.00	0.00	0.00	3,000.20
SNYDER LAKE	0.00	0.00	0.00	0.00	0.00	0.00	0.00	1,550.18	1,550.18
SPRINGWATER	0.00	0.00	0.00	0.00	0.00	0.00	0.00	640.00	640.00
STEWART LAKE	0.00	0.00	0.00	0.00	3.99	636.01	92,800.00	1,590.40	2,230.40
STONEY SLOUGH	0.00	0.00	0.00	0.00	0.00	0.00	0.00	880.00	880.00
STORM LAKE	0.00	0.00	0.00	0.00	0.00	1.70	161.00	684.20	685.90
STUMP LAKE	27.39	0.00	0.00	0.00	0.00	0.00	0.00	0.00	27.39
SULLYS HILL	1,673.85	0.00	0.00	0.00	0.00	0.00	0.00	1.29	1,675.14
SUNBURST LAKE	0.00	0.00	0.00	0.00	0.00	0.00	0.00	327.51	327.51
TEWAUKON	1.48	0.00	0.00	0.00	0.00	6,856.65	460,124.00	1,505.49	8,363.62
TOMAHAWK	0.00	0.00	0.00	0.00	0.00	0.00	0.00	440.00	440.00
UPPER SOURIS	160.17	0.00	28,758.43	0.00	7.36	3,159.99	41,220.00	216.30	32,302.25
WHITE LAKE	0.00	0.00	0.00	0.00	0.00	1,040.00	28,800.00	0.00	1,040.00
WILD RICE LAKE	0.00	0.00	0.00	0.00	0.00	0.00	0.00	778.80	778.80
WILLOW LAKE	0.00	0.00	0.00	0.00	.69	0.00	0.00	2,619.69	2,620.58
WINTERING RIVER	0.00	0.00	0.00	0.00	0.00	0.00	0.00	239.26	239.26
WOOD LAKE	0.00	0.00	0.00	0.00	0.00	0.00	0.00	280.00	280.00
STATE TOTAL 65	4,444.40	0.00	113,502.32	14,739.19	3,079.77	76,912.09	3,797,887.76	118,959.14	331,636.91
OHIO CEDAR POINT	0.00	0.00	0.00	0.00	2,445.42	0.00	0.00	4.35	2,449.77
OTTAWA	0.00	0.00	0.00	0.00	0.00	5,754.14	3,931,595.55	590.85	6,344.99
WEST SISTER ISLAND	77.13	0.00	0.00	0.00	0.00	0.00	0.00	3.00	80.13
STATE TOTAL 3	77.13	0.00	0.00	0.00	2,445.42	5,754.14	3,931,595.55	598.20	8,874.89
OKLAHOMA DEEP FORK	0.00	0.00	0.00	0.00	0.00	8,386.51	2,032,300.00	0.00	8,386.51
LITTLE RIVER	0.00	0.00	0.00	0.00	0.00	13,600.04	10,701,445.31	0.00	13,600.04
OPTIMA	0.00	0.00	0.00 E	4,332.81	0.00	0.00	0.00	0.00	4,332.81

Table 3 — National Wildlife Refuges

STATE AND UNIT	RESERVED FROM PUBLIC DOMAIN		ACQUIRED BY OTHER FEDERAL AGENCY		DEVISE OR GIFT	PURCHASED		AGREEMENT EASEMENT OR LEASE	TOTAL ACRES
	SOLE OR PRIMARY	SECONDARY	SOLE OR PRIMARY	SECONDARY		ACRES	COST ($)		
OKLAHOMA									
OZARK PLATEAU	0.00	0.00	255.00	0.00	420.00	2,558.04	587,165.00	403.53	3,636.57
SALT PLAINS	19,314.09	0.00	0.00	E 11,565.28	30.55	1,117.39	50,837.00	29.81	32,057.12
SEQUOYAH	0.00	0.00	0.00	E 20,800.00	0.00	0.00	0.00	0.00	20,800.00
TISHOMINGO	0.00	0.00	0.00	E 16,464.18	0.00	0.00	0.00	0.00	16,464.18
WASHITA	0.00	0.00	0.00	R 8,061.81	0.00	13.56	6,780.00	0.00	8,075.37
WICHITA MOUNTAINS	58,652.11	0.00	367.49	0.00	0.00	0.00	0.00	0.00	59,019.60
STATE TOTAL 9	77,966.20	0.00	622.49	61,224.08	450.55	25,675.54	13,378,527.31	433.34	166,372.20
OREGON									
ANKENY	0.00	0.00	0.00	0.00	0.00	2,796.33	893,600.00	0.00	2,796.33
BANDON MARSH	0.00	0.00	0.00	0.00	0.00	714.47	1,443,000.00	1.70	716.17
BASKETT SLOUGH	0.00	0.00	0.00	0.00	0.00	2,492.33	941,985.00	0.00	2,492.33
BEAR VALLEY	0.00	0.00	0.00	0.00	0.00	4,198.08	3,298,024.00	2.18	4,200.26
CAPE MEARES	138.51	0.00	0.00	0.00	0.00	0.00	0.00	0.00	138.51
COLD SPRINGS	50.00 R	1,748.15	0.00	R 951.80	0.00	386.88	2,760.00	0.00	3,116.83
DEER FLAT (21)*	162.44	0.00	0.00	0.00	0.00	0.00	0.00	0.00	162.44
FSA INTEREST OR ** *	0.00	0.00	269.00	0.00	0.00	0.00	0.00	338.05	607.05
HART MOUNTAIN	183,855.79	LM 1,951.76	837.95	0.00	606.16	82,671.92	2,814,274.58	0.00	269,923.58
JULIA BUTLER HANSEN (26)	0.00	0.00	0.00	0.00	136.03	2,367.74	2,150,510.00	249.61	2,753.38
KLAMATH MARSH	0.00	0.00	0.00	0.00	0.00	40,884.98	11,921,907.00	0.00	40,884.98
LEWIS AND CLARK	0.00	0.00	4,530.14	0.00	247.08	2,850.63	469,250.00	4.00	7,631.85
LOWER KLAMATH (2) *	6,550.63	0.00	0.00	0.00	67.50	0.00	0.00	0.00	6,618.13
MALHEUR	57,898.48	0.00	56,094.86	0.00	240.00	72,788.42	3,219,576.60	30.93	187,052.69
MCKAY CREEK	23.50	0.00	0.00	R 1,813.00	0.00	0.00	0.00	0.00	1,836.50
NESTUCCA BAY	0.00	0.00	30.70	0.00	0.00	619.94	1,524,403.00	0.00	650.64
OREGON ISLANDS	925.06	0.00	0.00	0.00	.41	151.82	2,580,000.00	2.32	1,079.61
SHELDON (15)*	0.00	0.00	0.00	0.00	0.00	627.48	4,079.00	0.00	627.48
SILETZ BAY	0.00	0.00	0.00	0.00	39.84	415.70	1,632,400.00	57.22	512.76
THREE ARCH ROCKS	15.00	0.00	0.00	0.00	0.00	0.00	0.00	0.00	15.00
TUALATIN RIVER	0.00	0.00	0.00	0.00	42.50	1,153.70	8,277,358.12	2.20	1,198.40
UMATILLA (26)	0.00 E	348.37	1,449.40	E 7,082.00	0.00	27.60	33,000.00	0.00	8,907.37
UPPER KLAMATH	10,655.31	0.00	0.00	0.00	0.00	4,310.85	123,476.00	0.00	14,966.16
WILLIAM L. FINLEY	0.00	0.00	0.00	0.00	0.00	5,665.96	2,480,800.00	7.15	5,673.11
STATE TOTAL 20	260,274.72	4,048.28	63,212.05	9,826.80	1,379.52	225,124.83	43,810,403.30	695.36	564,561.56
PENNSYLVANIA									
ERIE	0.00	0.00	0.00	0.00	0.00	8,777.21	1,595,755.64	0.00	8,777.21
JOHN HEINZ	0.00	0.00	87.26	0.00	243.14	662.77	8,146,763.80	0.00	993.17
OHIO RIVER ISLANDS (34)*	0.00	0.00	0.00	0.00	0.00	55.20	82,500.00	0.00	55.20
STATE TOTAL 2	0.00	0.00	87.26	0.00	243.14	9,495.18	9,825,019.44	0.00	9,825.58
RHODE ISLAND									
BLOCK ISLAND	0.00	0.00	26.30	0.00	0.00	82.62	5,505,000.00	20.00	128.92
JOHN H. CHAFEE	0.00	0.00	0.00	0.00	41.39	290.81	5,390,900.00	0.00	332.20
NINIGRET	0.00	0.00	398.66	0.00	0.00	299.61	3,588,000.00	.62	698.89
SACHUEST POINT	0.00	0.00	157.00	0.00	62.80	22.10	0.00	0.00	241.90
TRUSTOM POND	0.00	0.00	0.00	0.00	526.70	115.02	885,600.00	135.58	777.30
STATE TOTAL 5	0.00	0.00	581.96	0.00	630.89	810.16	15,369,500.00	156.20	2,179.21
SOUTH CAROLINA									
ACE BASIN	0.00	0.00	0.00	0.00	0.00	11,133.06	9,829,540.78	682.00	11,815.06
CAPE ROMAIN	0.00	0.00	5,242.36	0.00	6,496.42	22,306.16	53,768.18	31,180.00	65,224.94
CAROLINA SANDHILLS	0.00	0.00	44,106.73	0.00	0.00	1,241.70	42,852.75	0.00	45,348.43
FSA INTEREST SC ** *	0.00	0.00	200.30	0.00	0.00	0.00	0.00	1,229.74	1,430.04
PINCKNEY ISLAND	0.00	0.00	0.00	0.00	1,324.70	0.00	0.00	2,728.00	4,052.70

TABLE 3 - NATIONAL WILDLIFE REFUGES

STATE AND UNIT	RESERVED FROM PUBLIC DOMAIN		ACQUIRED BY OTHER FEDERAL AGENCY		DEVISE OR GIFT	PURCHASED		AGREEMENT EASEMENT OR LEASE	TOTAL ACRES
	SOLE OR PRIMARY	SECONDARY	SOLE OR PRIMARY	SECONDARY		ACRES	COST ($)		
SOUTH CAROLINA									
SANTEE	0.00	0.00	0.00	0.00	0.00	4,413.28	569,953.57	8,070.00	12,483.28
SAVANNAH (1) *	0.00	0.00	5,634.88	0.00	37.10	9,176.17	1,555,985.54	24.30	14,872.45
TYBEE	0.00	0.00	0.00 E	100.00	0.00	0.00	0.00	0.00	100.00
WACCAMAW	0.00	0.00	0.00	0.00	870.50	6,497.52	7,750,449.00	1.12	7,369.14
STATE TOTAL 7	0.00	0.00	55,184.27	100.00	8,728.72	54,767.89	19,802,499.82	43,915.16	162,696.04
SOUTH DAKOTA									
BEAR BUTTE	0.00	0.00	0.00	0.00	0.00	0.00	0.00	374.20	374.20
DAKOTA TALLGRASS PRAIRIE (44)*	0.00	0.00	0.00	0.00	0.00	0.00	0.00	25,539.93	25,539.93
FSA INTEREST SD ** *	0.00	0.00	0.00	0.00	0.00	0.00	0.00	151.20	151.20
KARL E. MUNDT (10)	0.00	0.00	0.00	0.00	738.82	0.00	0.00	305.00	1,043.82
LACREEK	0.00	0.00	6,807.47	0.00	223.11	9,379.75	788,491.00	445.00	16,855.33
LAKE ANDES	0.00	0.00	320.26	0.00	0.00	617.64	92,322.00	4,701.53	5,639.43
SAND LAKE	80.00	0.00	17,449.24	0.00	0.00	3,970.58	164,922.00	320.37	21,820.19
WAUBAY	0.00	0.00	3,965.92	0.00	0.00	683.77	25,836.00	90.53	4,740.22
STATE TOTAL 6	80.00	0.00	28,542.89	0.00	961.93	14,651.74	1,069,573.00	31,927.76	76,164.32
TENNESSEE									
CHICKASAW	0.00	0.00	0.00	0.00	0.00	17,951.81	17,989,310.00	5,387.90	23,339.71
CROSS CREEKS	0.00	0.00	6,327.77 E	2,442.00	0.00	91.72	26,200.00	0.00	8,861.49
FSA INTEREST TN ** *	0.00	0.00	112.98	0.00	0.00	0.00	0.00	572.41	685.39
HATCHIE	0.00	0.00	0.00	0.00	0.00	11,556.10	1,862,329.25	0.00	11,556.10
LAKE ISOM	0.00	0.00	1,485.12	0.00	0.00	360.84	27,290.72	0.00	1,845.96
LOWER HATCHIE	0.00	0.00	0.00	0.00	8.26	8,955.15	11,374,126.00	1,872.96	10,836.37
REELFOOT (22)*	0.00	0.00	0.00	0.00	0.00	563.43	279,531.78	7,847.31	8,410.74
TENNESSEE	0.00	0.00	0.00 T	50,830.30	0.00	527.67	247,147.10	1.49	51,359.46
STATE TOTAL 6	0.00	0.00	7,925.87	53,272.30	8.26	40,006.72	31,805,934.85	15,682.07	116,895.22
TEXAS									
ANAHUAC	0.00	0.00	0.00	0.00	352.57	33,880.57	13,871,963.67	63.09	34,296.23
ARANSAS	0.00	0.00	19,014.19	0.00	7,567.92	62,936.97	17,166,816.80	24,893.00	114,412.08
ATTWATER PRAIRIE CHICKEN	0.00	0.00	0.00	0.00	2,633.30	8,187.36	6,626,029.65	0.00	10,820.66
BALCONES CANYONLANDS	0.00	0.00	0.00	0.00	0.00	17,916.04	20,736,861.66	1,546.80	19,462.84
BIG BOGGY	0.00	0.00	0.00	0.00	0.00	4,216.29	2,457,398.19	309.88	4,526.17
BRAZORIA	0.00	0.00	0.00	0.00	25.00	44,220.20	14,664,988.26	168.68	44,413.88
BUFFALO LAKE	0.00	0.00	7,663.93	0.00	0.00	0.00	0.00	.23	7,664.16
CADDO LAKE	0.00	0.00	0.00 E	8,492.02	0.00	0.00	0.00	0.00	8,492.02
FSA INTEREST TX ** *	0.00	0.00	1,878.13	0.00	0.00	0.00	0.00	0.00	1,878.13
GRULLA (17)*	0.00	0.00	0.00	0.00	0.00	4.97	5,000.00	0.00	4.97
HAGERMAN	0.00	0.00	0.00 E	11,319.84	0.00	0.00	0.00	0.00	11,319.84
LAGUNA ATASCOSA	0.00	0.00	8,486.00	0.00	0.00	56,497.13	6,206,915.89	113.10	65,096.23
LITTLE SANDY	0.00	0.00	0.00	0.00	0.00	0.00	0.00	3,802.00	3,802.00
LOWER RIO GRANDE VALLEY	0.00	0.00	46.18	0.00	1,640.41	59,996.62	61,014,028.32	22,930.00	84,613.21
MCFADDIN	0.00	0.00	0.00	0.00	0.00	48,431.82	10,219,300.00	7,748.88	56,180.70
MOODY	0.00	0.00	0.00	0.00	0.00	0.00	0.00	3,516.87	3,516.87
MULESHOE	0.00	0.00	3,654.30	0.00	0.00	2,154.80	25,740.00	0.00	5,809.10
SAN BERNARD	0.00	0.00	0.00	0.00	1,184.90	32,344.64	10,528,605.19	127.00	33,656.54
SANTA ANA	0.00	0.00	0.00	0.00	37.06	2,049.91	203,519.00	.53	2,087.50
TEXAS POINT	0.00	0.00	0.00	0.00	0.00	8,952.02	1,719,000.00	0.00	8,952.02
TRINITY RIVER	0.00	0.00	0.00	0.00	0.00	12,920.08	7,410,570.00	0.00	12,920.08
STATE TOTAL 19	0.00	0.00	40,742.73	19,811.86	13,441.16	394,709.41	172,866,736.63	65,220.06	533,925.23
UTAH									
BEAR RIVER	43,442.89	0.00	0.00	0.00	4,272.21	25,883.64	2,888,119.47	46.64	73,645.38
COLORADO RIVER (46)	0.00	0.00	0.00	0.00	0.00	0.00	0.00	553.00	553.00

TABLE 3 - NATIONAL WILDLIFE REFUGES

STATE AND UNIT	RESERVED FROM PUBLIC DOMAIN		ACQUIRED BY OTHER FEDERAL AGENCY		DEVISE OR GIFT	PURCHASED		AGREEMENT EASEMENT OR LEASE	TOTAL ACRES
	SOLE OR PRIMARY	SECONDARY	SOLE OR PRIMARY	SECONDARY		ACRES	COST ($)		
UTAH									
FISH SPRINGS	14,217.42	0.00	0.00	0.00	0.00	3,774.82	93,525.00	0.00	17,992.24
FSA INTEREST UT ** *	0.00	0.00	0.00	0.00	0.00	0.00	0.00	280.84	280.84
OURAY	3,111.08	0.00	161.68	0.00	0.00	5,014.98	487,084.25	3,970.50	12,258.24
STATE TOTAL 4	60,771.39	0.00	161.68	0.00	4,272.21	34,673.44	3,468,528.72	4,850.98	104,729.70
VERMONT									
FSA INTEREST VT ** *	0.00	0.00	0.00	0.00	0.00	0.00	0.00	71.00	71.00
MISSISQUOI	0.00	0.00	0.00	0.00	264.50	6,256.98	291,134.27	0.00	6,521.48
SILVIO O. CONTE (41)	0.00	0.00	0.00	0.00	81.86	26,452.25	6,888,433.10	0.00	26,534.11
STATE TOTAL 2	0.00	0.00	0.00	0.00	346.36	32,709.23	7,179,567.37	71.00	33,126.59
VIRGINIA									
BACK BAY	0.00	0.00	0.00	0.00	2.36	8,800.56	21,865,185.08	0.00	8,802.92
CHINCOTEAGUE (23)	0.00	0.00	0.00	0.00	1,434.85	11,579.60	8,316,070.16	600.00	13,614.45
EASTERN SHORE OF VIRGINIA	0.00	0.00	175.33	0.00	70.35	872.32	3,882,445.00	5.27	1,123.27
FEATHERSTONE	0.00	0.00	0.00	0.00	161.92	163.90	486,800.00	0.00	325.82
FISHERMAN ISLAND	0.00	0.00	1,078.20	0.00	0.00	871.30	1,600,000.00	0.00	1,949.50
FSA INTEREST VA ** *	0.00	0.00	0.00	0.00	0.00	0.00	0.00	133.70	133.70
GREAT DISMAL SWAMP (24) *	0.00	0.00	27.14	0.00	49,097.01	35,968.96	17,198,270.15	0.00	85,093.11
JAMES RIVER	0.00	0.00	0.00	0.00	0.00	4,199.58	6,966,072.00	0.00	4,199.58
MACKAY ISLAND (24) *	0.00	0.00	0.00	0.00	0.00	874.40	26,855.75	0.00	874.40
MARTIN (25) *	0.00	0.00	0.00	0.00	145.62	0.00	0.00	0.00	145.62
MASON NECK	0.00	0.00	0.00	0.00	0.00	1,487.72	7,235,359.50	789.06	2,276.78
NANSEMOND	0.00	0.00	422.99	0.00	0.00	0.00	11,350.00	0.00	422.99
OCCOQUAN BAY	0.00	0.00	642.07	0.00	0.00	0.00	0.00	0.00	642.07
PLUM TREE ISLAND	0.00	0.00	3,275.60	0.00	15.08	211.00	105,500.00	0.00	3,501.68
PRESQUILE	0.00	0.00	0.00	0.00	1,328.92	0.00	0.00	0.00	1,328.92
RAPPAHANNOCK RIVER	0.00	0.00	0.00	0.00	1,338.84	3,353.35	7,451,756.00	44.12	4,736.31
WALLOPS ISLAND	0.00	0.00	373.00	0.00	0.00	0.00	0.00	3,000.00	3,373.00
STATE TOTAL 13	0.00	0.00	5,994.33	0.00	53,594.95	68,382.69	75,145,661.64	4,572.15	132,544.12
WASHINGTON									
COLUMBIA	10,978.11 R	1,387.11	(.00) R	1,274.89	0.00	15,062.09	458,001.04	894.07	29,596.27
CONBOY LAKE	0.00	0.00	0.00	0.00	0.00	6,186.56	2,356,600.00	718.29	6,904.85
COPALIS	60.80	0.00	0.00	0.00	0.00	0.00	0.00	0.00	60.80
DUNGENESS	202.50 CG	52.50	0.00	0.00	128.66	84.22	756,800.00	304.64	772.52
FLATTERY ROCKS	125.00	0.00	0.00	0.00	0.00	0.00	0.00	0.00	125.00
FRANZ LAKE	0.00	0.00	0.00	0.00	0.00	550.33	1,143,700.00	1.40	551.73
FSA INTEREST WA ** *	0.00	0.00	466.43	0.00	0.00	0.00	0.00	472.55	938.98
GRAYS HARBOR	0.00	0.00	0.00	0.00	0.00	1,407.77	1,039,800.00	63.61	1,471.38
JULIA BUTLER HANSEN (4) *	0.00	0.00	0.00	0.00	0.00	2,888.78	1,980,321.00	155.66	3,044.44
LITTLE PEND OREILLE	8,790.40	0.00	27,359.33	0.00	0.00	6,443.84	626,425.00	0.00	42,593.57
MCNARY	0.00	0.00	3,294.71 E	11,895.00	5.49	300.50	122,435.00	30.00	15,525.70
NISQUALLY	0.00	0.00	486.25	0.00	48.19	3,153.19	7,658,926.52	32.20	3,719.83
PIERCE	0.00	0.00	0.00	0.00	319.00	10.38	125,000.00	0.00	329.38
PROTECTION ISLAND	0.00	0.00	0.00	0.00	1.42	317.89	3,624,095.00	340.00	659.31
QUILLAYUTE NEEDLES	300.20	0.00	0.00	0.00	0.00	0.00	0.00	0.00	300.20
RIDGEFIELD	0.00	0.00	0.00	0.00	24.99	5,190.97	5,314,621.00	1.74	5,217.70
SADDLE MOUNTAIN	0.00 NR	440.00	0.00 NR	161,045.93	0.00	0.00	0.00	0.00	161,485.93
SAN JUAN ISLANDS	448.53	0.00	0.00	0.00	0.00	0.00	0.00	0.00	448.53
STEIGERWALD LAKE	0.00	0.00	652.44	0.00	0.00	413.58	2,763,000.00	0.00	1,046.02
TOPPENISH	0.00	0.00	0.00	0.00	0.00	1,977.55	715,137.00	1.29	1,978.84
TURNBULL	0.00	0.00	0.00	0.00	0.00	15,656.29	888,880.48	2,155.78	17,812.07
UMATILLA (4) *	0.00 E	102.50	1,465.83 E	13,107.00	0.00	0.00	0.00	200.50	14,875.83

TABLE 3 - NATIONAL WILDLIFE REFUGES

STATE AND UNIT	RESERVED FROM PUBLIC DOMAIN		ACQUIRED BY OTHER FEDERAL AGENCY		DEVISE OR GIFT	PURCHASED		AGREEMENT EASEMENT OR LEASE	TOTAL ACRES
	SOLE OR PRIMARY	SECONDARY	SOLE OR PRIMARY	SECONDARY		ACRES	COST ($)		
WASHINGTON WILLAPA	2,058.90	0.00	0.00	0.00	296.50	10,056.04	6,199,010.74	3,122.81	15,514.25
STATE TOTAL 20	22,964.44	1,962.11	33,704.99	187,322.82	824.25	69,679.98	35,772,252.78	8,514.54	324,973.13
WEST VIRGINIA CANAAN VALLEY	0.00	0.00	0.00	0.00	6.60	15,228.58	31,184,994.00	18.97	15,254.15
FSA INTEREST WV ** *	0.00	0.00	0.00	0.00	0.00	0.00	0.00	8.37	8.37
OHIO RIVER ISLANDS (35)	0.00	0.00	18.90	0.00	160.27	2,263.52	3,797,841.56	1.00	2,443.69
STATE TOTAL 2	0.00	0.00	18.90	0.00	166.87	17,492.10	34,982,835.56	28.34	17,706.21
WISCONSIN FOX RIVER	0.00	0.00	0.00	0.00	0.00	924.88	499,333.00	0.00	924.88
FSA INTEREST WI ** *	0.00	0.00	920.00	0.00	0.00	0.00	0.00	0.00	920.00
GRAVEL ISLAND	27.00	0.00	0.00	0.00	0.00	0.00	0.00	0.00	27.00
GREEN BAY	2.00	0.00	0.00	0.00	0.00	0.00	0.00	0.00	2.00
HORICON	0.00	0.00	0.00	0.00	5.44	21,142.58	709,987.42	33.83	21,181.85
NECEDAH	30.18	0.00	43,283.42	0.00	0.00	382.26	23,194.26	0.00	43,695.86
TREMPEALEAU	0.00	0.00	0.00	0.00	0.00	6,198.83	925,392.50	0.00	6,198.83
UPPER MISSISSIPPI RIVER (25)*	655.57	0.00	4.23 E	40,341.00	119.18	48,213.06	804,916.27	2.50	89,335.54
WHITTLESEY CREEK	0.00	0.00	0.00	0.00	50.02	67.79	236,000.00	0.00	117.81
STATE TOTAL 7	714.75	0.00	44,207.65	40,341.00	174.64	76,929.40	3,198,823.45	36.33	162,403.77
WYOMING BAMFORTH	201.23	0.00	0.00	0.00	0.00	964.80	6,368.00	0.00	1,166.03
COKEVILLE MEADOWS	0.00	0.00	0.00	0.00	0.00	5,793.82	2,637,912.76	2,793.50	8,587.32
FSA INTEREST WY ** *	0.00	0.00	0.00	0.00	0.00	0.00	0.00	3,132.75	3,132.75
HUTTON LAKE	152.85	0.00	0.00	0.00	0.00	1,815.49	7,943.00	0.00	1,968.34
MORTENSON LAKE	0.00	0.00	0.00	0.00	0.00	1,776.34	371,000.00	0.00	1,776.34
NATIONAL ELK	4,676.53	0.00	0.00	0.00	4,474.22	15,626.55	7,882,177.00	1.01	24,778.31
PATHFINDER	2,294.84 R	11,501.57	0.00 R	3,010.49	0.00	0.00	0.00	0.00	16,806.90
SEEDSKADEE	10,124.29	0.00	16,079.93	0.00	0.00	0.00	0.00	1,026.00	27,230.22
STATE TOTAL 7	17,449.74	11,501.57	16,079.93	3,010.49	4,474.22	25,977.00	10,905,400.76	6,953.26	85,446.21
AMERICAN SAMOA ROSE ATOLL	0.00	37,453.00	1,613.00	0.00	0.00	0.00	0.00	0.00	39,066.00
STATE TOTAL 1	0.00	37,453.00	1,613.00	0.00	0.00	0.00	0.00	0.00	39,066.00
BAKER ISLAND BAKER ISLAND	0.00	0.00	31,736.89	0.00	0.00	0.00	0.00	0.00	31,736.89
STATE TOTAL 1	0.00	0.00	31,736.89	0.00	0.00	0.00	0.00	0.00	31,736.89
GUAM GUAM	0.00	0.00	772.10	0.00	0.00	0.00	0.00	22,456.00	23,228.10
STATE TOTAL 1	0.00	0.00	772.10	0.00	0.00	0.00	0.00	22,456.00	23,228.10
HOWLAND ISLAND HOWLAND ISLAND	0.00	0.00	32,550.25	0.00	0.00	0.00	0.00	0.00	32,550.25
STATE TOTAL 1	0.00	0.00	32,550.25	0.00	0.00	0.00	0.00	0.00	32,550.25
JARVIS ISLAND JARVIS ISLAND	0.00	0.00	37,519.17	0.00	0.00	0.00	0.00	0.00	37,519.17
STATE TOTAL 1	0.00	0.00	37,519.17	0.00	0.00	0.00	0.00	0.00	37,519.17
JOHNSTON ATOLL JOHNSTON ISLAND	0.00	0.00	0.00	0.00	0.00	0.00	0.00	100.00	100.00
STATE TOTAL 1	0.00	0.00	0.00	0.00	0.00	0.00	0.00	100.00	100.00
KINGMAN REEF KINGMAN REEF	0.00	0.00	426,392.00	0.00	0.00	0.00	0.00	0.00	426,392.00
STATE TOTAL 1	0.00	0.00	426,392.00	0.00	0.00	0.00	0.00	0.00	426,392.00

TABLE 3 - NATIONAL WILDLIFE REFUGES

STATE AND UNIT	RESERVED FROM PUBLIC DOMAIN		ACQUIRED BY OTHER FEDERAL AGENCY		DEVISE OR GIFT	PURCHASED		AGREEMENT EASEMENT OR LEASE	TOTAL ACRES
	SOLE OR PRIMARY	SECONDARY	SOLE OR PRIMARY	SECONDARY		ACRES	COST ($)		
MIDWAY ISLANDS MIDWAY ATOLL	0.00	0.00	298,362.30	0.00	0.00	0.00	0.00	0.00	298,362.30
STATE TOTAL 1	0.00	0.00	298,362.30	0.00	0.00	0.00	0.00	0.00	298,362.30
NAVASSA ISLAND NAVASSA ISLAND	0.00	0.00	364,950.00	0.00	0.00	0.00	0.00	0.00	364,950.00
STATE TOTAL 1	0.00	0.00	364,950.00	0.00	0.00	0.00	0.00	0.00	364,950.00
PALMYRA ATOLL PALMYRA ATOLL	0.00	0.00	504,576.00	0.00	0.00	0.00	0.00	0.00	504,576.00
STATE TOTAL 1	0.00	0.00	504,576.00	0.00	0.00	0.00	0.00	0.00	504,576.00
PUERTO RICO CABO ROJO	0.00	0.00	587.33	0.00	0.00	1,270.00	2,999,265.63	0.00	1,857.33
CULEBRA	0.00	0.00	1,478.35 N	68.00	0.00	0.00	0.00	14.21	1,560.56
DESECHEO	0.00	0.00	360.00	0.00	0.00	0.00	0.00	0.00	360.00
LAGUNA CARTAGENA	0.00	0.00	262.86	0.00	0.00	0.00	0.00	772.89	1,035.75
PUERTO RICO VIEQUES	0.00	0.00	3,100.00	0.00	0.00	0.00	0.00	0.00	3,100.00
STATE TOTAL 5	0.00	0.00	5,788.54	68.00	0.00	1,270.00	2,999,265.63	787.10	7,913.64
VIRGIN ISLANDS BUCK ISLAND	0.00	0.00	45.15	0.00	0.00	0.00	0.00	0.00	45.15
GREEN CAY	0.00	0.00	0.00	0.00	0.00	13.77	250,000.00	0.00	13.77
SANDY POINT	0.00	0.00	0.00	0.00	0.00	512.17	3,132,470.00	0.00	512.17
STATE TOTAL 3	0.00	0.00	45.15	0.00	0.00	525.94	3,382,470.00	0.00	571.09
GRAND TOTAL 540	81,301,616.64	713,174.61	3,115,807.54	941,661.35	703,140.82	4,054,794.60	1,662,780,890.69	1,273,885.82	92,104,081.38

(1) ALSO IN GEORGIA
(2) ALSO IN CALIFORNIA
(3) ALSO IN ARIZONA
(4) ALSO IN OREGON
(5) ALSO IN ALABAMA
(6) ALSO IN FLORIDA
(7) ALSO IN SOUTH CAROLINA
(8) ALSO IN MISSOURI
(9) ALSO IN IOWA, MINNESOTA AND WISCONSIN
(10) ALSO IN NEBRASKA
(11) ALSO IN ILLINOIS
(12) ALSO IN TEXAS
(13) ALSO IN ILLINOIS, MINNESOTA, AND WISCONSIN
(14) ALSO IN TENNESSEE
(15) ALSO IN NEVADA
(16) ALSO IN VIRGINIA
(17) ALSO IN NEW MEXICO
(18) ALSO IN ILLINOIS, IOWA, AND WISCONSIN
(19) ALSO IN IOWA
(20) ALSO IN SOUTH DAKOTA
(21) ALSO IN IDAHO
(22) ALSO IN KENTUCKY
(23) ALSO IN MARYLAND
(24) ALSO IN NORTH CAROLINA
(25) ALSO IN ILLINOIS, IOWA, AND MINNESOTA
(26) ALSO IN WASHINGTON
(27) ALSO IN MISSISSIPPI
(28) ALSO IN LOUISIANA
(33) ALSO IN ILLINOIS AND IOWA
(34) ALSO IN WEST VIRGINIA AND KENTUCKY
(35) ALSO IN PENNSYLVANIA AND KENTUCKY
(36) ALSO IN NEW HAMPSHIRE
(37) ALSO IN MAINE
(38) ALSO IN WEST VIRGINIA AND PENNSYLVANIA
(39) ALSO IN NEW YORK
(40) ALSO IN NEW JERSEY
(41) ALSO IN MASSACHUSETTS AND NEW HAMPSHIRE
(42) ALSO IN VERMONT AND NEW HAMPSHIRE
(43) ALSO IN VERMONT AND MASSACHUSETTS
(44) ALSO IN NORTH DAKOTA
(45) ALSO IN UTAH
(46) ALSO IN COLORADO
(47) ALSO IN MINNESOTA

A   - DEPARTMENT OF THE ARMY
BIA - BUREAU OF INDIAN AFFAIRS, DEPARTMENT OF THE INTERIOR
C   - DEPARTMENT OF COMMERCE
CG   - COAST GUARD, DEPARTMENT OF TRANSPORTATION
E   - CORPS OF ENGINEERS, DEPARTMENT OF THE ARMY
F   - FOREST SERVICE, DEPARTMENT OF AGRICULTURE
FA   - FEDERAL AVIATION ADMINISTRATION, DEPARTMENT OF TRANSPORTATION
FSA - FARM SERVICE AGENCY (FORMERLY FARMERS HOME ADMINISTRATION, DEPARTMENT OF AGRICULTURE)
GS   - GEOLOGICAL SURVEY
LM   - BUREAU OF LAND MANAGEMENT, DEPARTMENT OF THE INTERIOR
MMS - MINERALS MANAGEMENT SERVICE, DEPARTMENT OF THE INTERIOR
N   - DEPARTMENT OF THE NAVY
NA   - NATIONAL AERONAUTICS AND SPACE ADMINISTRATION
NR   - NUCLEAR REGULATORY COMMISSION
R   - BUREAU OF REGULATORY COMMISSION
T   - TENNESSEE VALLEY AUTHORITY

(#)* - COUNTED IN ANOTHER STATE

** * - SUMMARY BY STATE OF ALL OTHER ACRES, BOTH FEE AND LESS THAN FEE, ACQUIRED FROM THE
        FSA (FORMERLY FARMERS HOME ADMINISTRATION), NOT REPORTED WITHIN AN EXISTING PROJECT.
        SUMMARY MAY CONTAIN ONE OR MORE OWNERSHIPS. FSA INTEREST STATE SUMMARY ACRES ARE
        INCLUDED IN THE TOTAL ACRES FOR EACH STATE BUT ARE NOT COUNTED AS SEPARATE UNITS IN
        THE NATIONAL WILDLIFE REFUGE STATE TOTALS.

TABLE 4 - WATERFOWL PRODUCTION AREA COUNTIES

STATE AND UNIT		RESERVED FROM PUBLIC DOMAIN		ACQUIRED BY OTHER FEDERAL AGENCY		DEVISE OR GIFT	PURCHASED		AGREEMENT EASEMENT OR LEASE	TOTAL ACRES
		SOLE OR PRIMARY	SECONDARY	SOLE OR PRIMARY	SECONDARY		ACRES	COST ($)		
IDAHO										
OXFORD SLOUGH		0.00	0.00	0.00	0.00	0.00	1,878.41	530,000.00	0.00	1,878.41
WMD TOTAL	1	0.00	0.00	0.00	0.00	0.00	1,878.41	530,000.00	0.00	1,878.41
STATE TOTAL	1	0.00	0.00	0.00	0.00	0.00	1,878.41	530,000.00	0.00	1,878.41
IOWA										
IOWA WMD BOONE		0.00	0.00	0.00	0.00	0.00	391.33	599,600.00	0.00	391.33
BUENA VISTA		0.00	0.00	0.00	0.00	0.00	69.09	169,000.00	0.00	69.09
CERRO GORDO		0.00	0.00	0.00	0.00	0.00	2,494.25	2,832,677.82	5.70	2,499.95
CLAY		0.00	0.00	0.00	0.00	0.00	709.19	852,206.85	0.00	709.19
DICKINSON		0.00	0.00	0.00	0.00	.65	4,895.82	5,897,157.00	98.00	4,994.47
EMMET		0.00	0.00	0.00	0.00	0.00	1,653.84	2,081,075.00	58.00	1,711.84
GREENE		0.00	0.00	0.00	0.00	0.00	669.05	1,260,700.00	0.00	669.05
GUTHRIE		0.00	0.00	0.00	0.00	0.00	185.53	293,840.00	0.00	185.53
HANCOCK		0.00	0.00	0.00	0.00	0.00	802.70	545,480.26	7.00	809.70
KOSSUTH		0.00	0.00	0.00	0.00	0.00	2,013.65	3,480,438.23	23.00	2,036.65
OSCEOLA		0.00	0.00	0.00	0.00	0.00	0.00	0.00	41.00	41.00
PALO ALTO		0.00	0.00	0.00	0.00	0.00	627.56	844,092.65	282.00	909.56
POCAHONTAS		0.00	0.00	0.00	0.00	0.00	223.76	455,000.00	0.00	223.76
POLK		0.00	0.00	0.00	0.00	0.00	110.00	241,500.00	0.00	110.00
SAC		0.00	0.00	0.00	0.00	0.00	296.52	363,880.00	0.00	296.52
WINNEBAGO		0.00	0.00	0.00	0.00	0.00	1,023.15	1,138,300.31	105.00	1,128.15
WORTH		0.00	0.00	0.00	0.00	0.00	1,491.84	1,088,329.87	18.00	1,509.84
WRIGHT		0.00	0.00	0.00	0.00	0.00	1,528.09	2,228,025.00	0.00	1,528.09
WMD TOTAL	18	0.00	0.00	0.00	0.00	.65	19,185.37	24,371,282.99	637.70	19,823.72
STATE TOTAL	18	0.00	0.00	0.00	0.00	.65	19,185.37	24,371,282.99	637.70	19,823.72
MAINE										
CARLTON POND		0.00	0.00	0.00	0.00	0.00	1,068.21	18,276.08	0.00	1,068.21
WMD TOTAL	1	0.00	0.00	0.00	0.00	0.00	1,068.21	18,276.08	0.00	1,068.21
STATE TOTAL	1	0.00	0.00	0.00	0.00	0.00	1,068.21	18,276.08	0.00	1,068.21
MICHIGAN										
MICHIGAN WMD JACKSON		0.00	0.00	0.00	0.00	0.00	160.00	170,000.00	0.00	160.00
VAN BUREN		0.00	0.00	0.00	0.00	0.00	77.08	43,600.00	0.00	77.08
WMD TOTAL	2	0.00	0.00	0.00	0.00	0.00	237.08	213,600.00	0.00	237.08
STATE TOTAL	2	0.00	0.00	0.00	0.00	0.00	237.08	213,600.00	0.00	237.08
MINNESOTA										
BIG STONE WMD LINCOLN		0.00	0.00	0.00	0.00	0.00	754.26	423,650.00	517.37	1,271.63
LYON		0.00	0.00	0.00	0.00	0.00	1,553.56	1,269,720.00	280.80	1,834.36
WMD TOTAL	2	0.00	0.00	0.00	0.00	0.00	2,307.82	1,693,370.00	798.17	3,105.99
DETROIT LAKES WMD BECKER		0.00	0.00	0.00	0.00	4.33	11,763.18	3,162,020.56	2,012.14	13,779.65
CLAY		0.00	0.00	0.00	0.00	0.00	10,385.89	2,979,545.18	3,338.42	13,724.31
MAHNOMEN		0.00	0.00	0.00	0.00	0.00	5,399.33	853,558.90	4,947.00	10,346.33
NORMAN		0.00	0.00	0.00	0.00	0.00	1,120.00	400,000.00	0.00	1,120.00
POLK		0.00	0.00	0.00	0.00	0.00	11,537.35	2,169,752.86	1,743.80	13,281.15
WMD TOTAL	5	0.00	0.00	0.00	0.00	4.33	40,205.75	9,564,877.50	12,041.36	52,251.44

TABLE 4 - WATERFOWL PRODUCTION AREA COUNTIES

STATE AND UNIT	RESERVED FROM PUBLIC DOMAIN		ACQUIRED BY OTHER FEDERAL AGENCY		DEVISE OR GIFT	PURCHASED		AGREEMENT EASEMENT OR LEASE	TOTAL ACRES
	SOLE OR PRIMARY	SECONDARY	SOLE OR PRIMARY	SECONDARY		ACRES	COST ($)		
MINNESOTA									
FERGUS FALLS WMD									
DOUGLAS	0.00	0.00	0.00	0.00	0.00	9,605.07	1,916,515.20	6,128.24	15,733.31
GRANT	0.00	0.00	0.00	0.00	0.00	10,050.83	2,669,508.12	3,607.10	13,657.93
OTTER TAIL	0.00	0.00	0.00	0.00	52.19	20,854.48	6,879,052.26	14,026.43	34,933.10
WILKIN	0.00	0.00	0.00	0.00	0.00	2,196.43	702,564.35	309.00	2,505.43
WMD TOTAL 4	0.00	0.00	0.00	0.00	52.19	42,706.81	12,167,639.93	24,070.77	66,829.77
LITCHFIELD WMD									
AITKIN	0.00	0.00	0.00	0.00	0.00	69.86	28,000.00	0.00	69.86
KANDIYOHI	0.00	0.00	0.00	0.00	0.00	13,226.56	4,980,725.93	4,264.83	17,491.39
MCLEOD	0.00	0.00	0.00	0.00	0.00	951.66	1,136,793.00	739.27	1,690.93
MEEKER	0.00	0.00	0.00	0.00	0.00	4,708.99	3,972,224.10	2,258.14	6,967.13
RENVILLE	0.00	0.00	0.00	0.00	0.00	1,133.03	1,396,340.00	0.00	1,133.03
STEARNS	0.00	0.00	0.00	0.00	0.00	9,069.71	2,710,733.87	1,516.33	10,586.04
TODD	0.00	0.00	0.00	0.00	0.00	802.85	385,672.20	16.00	818.85
WRIGHT	0.00	0.00	0.00	0.00	0.00	2,500.92	2,527,820.90	437.50	2,938.42
WMD TOTAL 8	0.00	0.00	0.00	0.00	0.00	32,463.58	17,138,310.00	9,232.07	41,695.65
MINNESOTA VALLEY WMD									
BLUE EARTH	0.00	0.00	0.00	0.00	0.00	946.93	1,331,100.00	78.70	1,025.63
CARVER	0.00	0.00	0.00	0.00	0.00	219.00	321,000.00	47.57	266.57
DAKOTA	0.00	0.00	0.00	0.00	0.00	73.90	201,747.00	.05	73.95
LESUEUR	0.00	0.00	0.00	0.00	0.00	413.79	539,254.50	209.15	622.94
RICE	0.00	0.00	0.00	0.00	0.00	412.10	631,999.35	370.74	782.84
SCOTT	0.00	0.00	0.00	0.00	0.00	40.00	109,200.00	164.21	204.21
SIBLEY	0.00	0.00	0.00	0.00	43.48	862.40	1,079,789.73	253.25	1,159.13
STEELE	0.00	0.00	0.00	0.00	0.00	630.11	653,244.00	0.00	630.11
WASECA	0.00	0.00	0.00	0.00	0.00	248.78	408,000.00	0.00	248.78
WMD TOTAL 9	0.00	0.00	0.00	0.00	43.48	3,847.01	5,275,334.58	1,123.67	5,014.16
MORRIS WMD									
BIG STONE	0.00	0.00	0.00	0.00	0.00	11,502.69	2,294,645.83	8,065.43	19,568.12
CHIPPEWA	0.00	0.00	0.00	0.00	0.00	244.10	127,050.00	57.00	301.10
LAC QUI PARLE	0.00	0.00	0.00	0.00	0.00	4,007.42	986,028.73	1,657.07	5,664.49
POPE	0.00	0.00	0.00	0.00	80.00	12,684.11	2,473,445.07	8,913.08	21,677.19
STEVENS	0.00	0.00	0.00	0.00	0.00	9,596.93	3,463,202.84	1,206.00	10,802.93
SWIFT	0.00	0.00	0.00	0.00	0.00	7,601.12	1,804,930.17	1,844.87	9,445.99
TRAVERSE	0.00	0.00	0.00	0.00	0.00	4,105.55	1,469,568.63	1,284.45	5,390.00
YELLOW MEDICINE	0.00	0.00	0.00	0.00	0.00	959.58	703,683.30	235.09	1,194.67
WMD TOTAL 8	0.00	0.00	0.00	0.00	80.00	50,901.50	13,322,574.57	23,262.99	74,244.49
TAMARAC WMD									
CASS	0.00	0.00	0.00	0.00	0.00	0.00	0.00	43.00	43.00
CLEARWATER	0.00	0.00	0.00	0.00	0.00	0.00	0.00	864.00	864.00
WMD TOTAL 2	0.00	0.00	0.00	0.00	0.00	0.00	0.00	907.00	907.00
WINDOM WMD									
COTTONWOOD	0.00	0.00	0.00	0.00	0.00	2,945.14	1,380,053.85	192.85	3,137.99
FARIBAULT	0.00	0.00	0.00	0.00	0.00	830.06	800,991.80	129.37	959.43
FREEBORN	0.00	0.00	0.00	0.00	0.00	1,631.99	1,833,367.25	143.26	1,775.25
JACKSON	0.00	0.00	0.00	0.00	0.00	4,169.56	2,885,810.28	383.09	4,552.65
MARTIN	0.00	0.00	0.00	0.00	0.00	70.89	45,369.60	271.65	342.54
MURRAY	0.00	0.00	0.00	0.00	0.00	1,921.18	2,265,977.00	21.00	1,942.18
NOBLES	0.00	0.00	0.00	0.00	0.00	521.65	580,802.00	26.00	547.65
ROCK	0.00	0.00	0.00	0.00	0.00	0.00	0.00	11.00	11.00
WATONWAN	0.00	0.00	0.00	0.00	0.00	56.65	31,157.50	168.42	225.07
WMD TOTAL 9	0.00	0.00	0.00	0.00	0.00	12,147.12	9,773,529.28	1,346.64	13,493.76

31

TABLE 4 - WATERFOWL PRODUCTION AREA COUNTIES

STATE AND UNIT	RESERVED FROM PUBLIC DOMAIN		ACQUIRED BY OTHER FEDERAL AGENCY		DEVISE OR GIFT	PURCHASED		AGREEMENT EASEMENT OR LEASE	TOTAL ACRES
	SOLE OR PRIMARY	SECONDARY	SOLE OR PRIMARY	SECONDARY		ACRES	COST ($)		
MINNESOTA									
WINDOM WMD									
STATE TOTAL 47	0.00	0.00	0.00	0.00	180.00	184,579.59	68,935,635.86	72,782.67	257,542.26
MONTANA									
BENTON LAKE WMD CASCADE	0.00	0.00	0.00	0.00	0.00	727.46	299,606.00	78.00	805.46
CHOUTEAU	0.00	0.00	0.00	0.00	0.00	2,156.13	538,543.00	501.00	2,657.13
GLACIER	0.00	0.00	0.00	0.00	0.00	94.20	17,898.00	9,818.33	9,912.53
HILL	0.00	0.00	0.00	0.00	378.93	0.00	0.00	918.00	1,296.93
LEWIS AND CLARK	0.00	0.00	0.00	0.00	0.00	0.00	0.00	1,845.50	1,845.50
LIBERTY	0.00	0.00	0.00	0.00	0.00	0.00	0.00	428.00	428.00
PONDERA	0.00	0.00	0.00	0.00	0.00	640.00	93,000.00	8,487.01	9,127.01
POWELL	0.00	0.00	0.00	0.00	1,802.07	2,644.60	828,834.00	22,608.41	27,055.08
TETON *	0.00	0.00	0.00	0.00	0.00	1,486.05	376,253.00	5,100.46	6,586.51
TOOLE	0.00	0.00	0.00	0.00	0.00	4,329.18	983,964.00	12,166.37	16,495.55
WMD TOTAL 10	0.00	0.00	0.00	0.00	2,181.00	12,057.62	3,138,098.00	61,951.08	76,189.70
BOWDOIN WMD BLAINE	0.00	0.00	0.00	0.00	0.00	2,435.26	167,340.00	2,604.20	5,039.46
PHILLIPS	0.00	0.00	0.00	0.00	0.00	6,328.83	1,206,863.00	24,372.55	30,701.38
VALLEY	0.00	0.00	0.00	0.00	0.00	0.00	0.00	201.00	201.00
WMD TOTAL 3	0.00	0.00	0.00	0.00	0.00	8,764.09	1,374,203.00	27,177.75	35,941.84
CHARLES M. RUSSELL WMD GOLDEN VALLEY	0.00	0.00	0.00	0.00	0.00	760.27	76,427.00	160.00	920.27
MUSSELSHELL	0.00	0.00	0.00	0.00	0.00	532.45	163,001.00	160.00	692.45
PETROLEUM	0.00	0.00	0.00	0.00	0.00	40.00	23,800.00	0.00	40.00
STILLWATER	0.00	0.00	0.00	0.00	0.00	1,828.10	207,625.00	.38	1,828.48
YELLOWSTONE	0.00	0.00	0.00	0.00	0.00	486.42	55,600.00	0.00	486.42
WMD TOTAL 5	0.00	0.00	0.00	0.00	0.00	3,647.24	526,453.00	320.38	3,967.62
NORTHEAST MONTANA WMD DANIELS	0.00	0.00	0.00	0.00	7.85	1,080.58	97,669.00	1,011.32	2,099.75
ROOSEVELT	0.00	0.00	0.00	0.00	0.00	179.20	14,000.00	7,402.42	7,581.62
SHERIDAN	39.10	0.00	0.00	0.00	0.00	10,491.58	1,244,031.08	10,231.16	20,761.84
WMD TOTAL 3	39.10	0.00	0.00	0.00	7.85	11,751.36	1,355,700.08	18,644.90	30,443.21
NORTHWEST MONTANA WMD FLATHEAD	0.00	0.00	0.00	0.00	807.92	4,410.31	2,246,518.00	0.00	5,218.23
LAKE	0.00	0.00	0.00	0.00	0.00	3,228.36	2,306,855.00	4,185.69	7,414.05
WMD TOTAL 2	0.00	0.00	0.00	0.00	807.92	7,638.67	4,553,373.00	4,185.69	12,632.28
STATE TOTAL 23	39.10	0.00	0.00	0.00	2,996.77	43,858.98	10,947,827.08	112,279.80	159,174.65
NEBRASKA									
RAINWATER BASIN WMD ADAMS	0.00	0.00	0.00	0.00	163.00	231.56	230,000.00	160.00	554.56
CLAY	0.00	0.00	1,052.19	0.00	0.00	5,308.14	2,348,258.85	4.25	6,364.58
FILLMORE	0.00	0.00	0.00	0.00	0.00	3,337.60	1,631,453.00	6.60	3,344.20
FRANKLIN	0.00	0.00	0.00	0.00	157.36	1,625.96	402,698.00	0.00	1,783.32
GOSPER	0.00	0.00	0.00	0.00	0.00	1,451.50	233,923.00	0.00	1,451.50
HALL *	0.00	0.00	320.70	0.00	0.00	328.77	435,000.00	0.00	649.47
HAMILTON *	0.00	0.00	160.00	0.00	80.00	880.00	1,271,250.00	6.00	1,126.00
KEARNEY *	0.00	0.00	0.00	0.00	0.00	2,874.43	657,681.00	175.50	3,049.93
PHELPS	0.00	0.00	0.00	0.00	0.00	4,595.14	3,573,111.00	0.00	4,595.14
POLK FSA ** *	0.00	0.00	0.00	0.00	0.00	0.00	0.00	140.78	140.78
SALINE FSA ** *	0.00	0.00	61.35	0.00	0.00	0.00	0.00	43.00	104.35
SEWARD	0.00	0.00	0.00	0.00	0.00	471.14	309,010.45	0.00	471.14

TABLE 4 - WATERFOWL PRODUCTION AREA COUNTIES

STATE AND UNIT	RESERVED FROM PUBLIC DOMAIN		ACQUIRED BY OTHER FEDERAL AGENCY		DEVISE OR GIFT	PURCHASED		AGREEMENT EASEMENT OR LEASE	TOTAL ACRES
	SOLE OR PRIMARY	SECONDARY	SOLE OR PRIMARY	SECONDARY		ACRES	COST ($)		
NEBRASKA									
RAINWATER BASIN WMD									
YORK *	0.00	0.00	0.00	0.00	0.00	879.20	419,429.00	41.00	920.20
WMD TOTAL 11	0.00	0.00	1,594.24	0.00	400.36	21,983.44	11,509,814.50	577.13	24,555.17
STATE TOTAL 11	0.00	0.00	1,594.24	0.00	400.36	21,983.44	11,509,814.50	577.13	24,555.17
NORTH DAKOTA									
ARROWWOOD WMD									
EDDY *	29.84	0.00	0.00	0.00	0.00	4,627.21	498,001.00	12,227.13	16,884.18
FOSTER	0.00	0.00	0.00	0.00	0.00	1,487.07	96,568.00	6,828.00	8,515.07
WMD TOTAL 2	29.84	0.00	0.00	0.00	0.00	6,114.28	594,569.00	19,055.13	25,199.25
AUDUBON WMD									
HETTINGER	0.00	0.00	1,202.60	0.00	0.00	0.00	0.00	0.00	1,202.60
MCLEAN	515.00	0.00	7,600.91	0.00	159.00	4,068.29	420,234.00	24,941.91	37,285.11
SHERIDAN *	229.20	0.00	3,999.13	0.00	334.49	7,661.50	468,427.00	41,020.45	53,244.77
WARD	120.00	0.00	0.00	0.00	0.00	5,868.09	489,211.00	43,281.98	49,270.07
WMD TOTAL 4	864.20	0.00	12,802.64	0.00	493.49	17,597.88	1,377,872.00	109,244.34	141,002.55
CHASE LAKE PRAIRIE PROJECT WMD									
STUTSMAN *	251.66	0.00	1,562.69	0.00	0.00	26,462.64	1,667,016.00	52,175.42	80,452.41
WELLS *	0.00	0.00	2,935.40	0.00	0.00	7,661.43	1,188,559.00	13,590.40	24,187.23
WMD TOTAL 2	251.66	0.00	4,498.09	0.00	0.00	34,124.07	2,855,575.00	65,765.82	104,639.64
CROSBY WMD									
BURKE	0.00	0.00	0.00	0.00	0.00	3,544.19	180,068.00	41,287.58	44,831.77
DIVIDE	1,244.83	0.00	0.00	0.00	0.00	9,444.62	474,790.00	34,647.09	45,336.54
WILLIAMS *	320.00	0.00	0.00	0.00	0.00	4,163.17	278,057.00	8,584.00	13,067.17
WMD TOTAL 3	1,564.83	0.00	0.00	0.00	0.00	17,151.98	932,915.00	84,518.67	103,235.48
DEVILS LAKE WMD									
BENSON *	1,660.85	0.00	232.15	0.00	0.00	7,322.66	607,908.00	38,474.67	47,690.33
CAVALIER *	0.00	0.00	723.71	0.00	0.00	10,129.12	1,354,471.00	13,910.00	24,762.83
GRAND FORKS	18.30	0.00	0.00	0.00	21.77	6,195.27	1,279,208.85	1,505.90	7,741.24
NELSON *	0.00	0.00	340.91	0.00	0.00	3,203.23	174,341.00	38,322.20	41,866.34
PEMBINA *	0.00	0.00	0.00	0.00	0.00	2,258.56	218,678.00	391.30	2,649.86
RAMSEY *	132.10	0.00	1,119.43	0.00	0.00	8,225.00	1,144,252.00	29,116.00	38,592.53
TOWNER *	13.50	0.00	829.39	0.00	641.05	3,837.02	494,146.00	25,165.00	30,485.96
WALSH *	5.50	0.00	387.52	0.00	0.00	1,393.19	98,128.00	9,096.61	10,882.82
WMD TOTAL 8	1,830.25	0.00	3,633.11	0.00	662.82	42,564.05	5,371,132.85	155,981.68	204,671.91
J. CLARK SALYER WMD									
BOTTINEAU *	7.40	0.00	210.30	0.00	0.00	2,371.47	200,763.00	29,408.14	31,997.31
MCHENRY *	993.59	0.00	0.00	0.00	0.00	4,888.80	374,404.50	43,123.90	49,006.29
PIERCE *	3,276.00	0.00	1,054.56	0.00	1.20	8,417.74	922,115.00	41,620.61	54,370.11
RENVILLE	0.00	0.00	0.00	0.00	0.00	311.09	23,523.00	15,403.60	15,714.69
ROLETTE	105.96	0.00	0.00	0.00	0.00	5,694.03	759,347.00	20,510.01	26,310.00
WMD TOTAL 5	4,382.95	0.00	1,264.86	0.00	1.20	21,683.13	2,280,152.50	150,066.26	177,398.40
KULM WMD									
DICKEY *	306.75	0.00	0.00	0.00	0.00	9,735.40	1,150,816.00	37,972.34	48,014.49
LA MOURE *	0.00	0.00	634.89	0.00	0.00	4,799.96	505,095.00	14,076.70	19,511.55
LOGAN *	835.00	0.00	160.03	0.00	0.00	11,226.24	1,006,598.00	40,287.11	52,508.38
MCINTOSH *	297.58	0.00	0.00	0.00	9.60	17,373.48	1,368,865.00	30,023.90	47,704.56
WMD TOTAL 4	1,439.33	0.00	794.92	0.00	9.60	43,135.08	4,031,374.00	122,360.05	167,738.98
LONG LAKE WMD									
BURLEIGH *	850.10	0.00	794.69	0.00	0.00	9,611.44	1,949,864.00	30,528.96	41,785.19
EMMONS *	480.00	0.00	0.00	0.00	0.00	3,135.29	174,321.75	11,800.60	15,415.89
KIDDER *	1,769.79	0.00	0.00	0.00	0.00	5,633.88	438,439.00	67,335.01	74,738.68

TABLE 4 — WATERFOWL PRODUCTION AREA COUNTIES

STATE AND UNIT		RESERVED FROM PUBLIC DOMAIN		ACQUIRED BY OTHER FEDERAL AGENCY		DEVISE OR GIFT	PURCHASED		AGREEMENT EASEMENT OR LEASE	TOTAL ACRES
		SOLE OR PRIMARY	SECONDARY	SOLE OR PRIMARY	SECONDARY		ACRES	COST ($)		
NORTH DAKOTA										
LONG LAKE WMD										
WMD TOTAL	3	3,099.89	0.00	794.69	0.00	0.00	18,380.61	2,562,624.75	109,664.57	131,939.76
LOSTWOOD WMD MOUNTRAIL	*	467.52	0.00	400.00	0.00	0.00	10,155.10	940,661.00	43,078.10	54,100.72
WMD TOTAL	1	467.52	0.00	400.00	0.00	0.00	10,155.10	940,661.00	43,078.10	54,100.72
TEWAUKON WMD RANSOM		0.00	0.00	0.00	0.00	0.00	4,315.02	617,357.00	23,194.06	27,509.08
RICHLAND		0.00	0.00	0.00	0.00	0.00	5,992.25	938,052.00	5,956.80	11,949.05
SARGENT	*	0.00	0.00	405.71	0.00	0.00	3,537.46	305,439.00	21,005.08	24,948.25
WMD TOTAL	3	0.00	0.00	405.71	0.00	0.00	13,844.73	1,860,848.00	50,155.94	64,406.38
VALLEY CITY WMD BARNES	*	1.26	0.00	338.63	0.00	15.61	6,661.68	958,087.00	18,999.70	26,016.88
CASS		0.00	0.00	0.00	0.00	0.00	3,424.81	623,044.00	1,759.90	5,184.71
GRIGGS		158.05	0.00	0.00	0.00	0.00	3,069.46	373,990.00	16,742.00	19,969.51
STEELE		0.00	0.00	0.00	0.00	0.00	3,249.25	538,345.00	4,383.30	7,632.55
TRAILL		0.00	0.00	0.00	0.00	0.00	719.25	75,109.00	234.00	953.25
WMD TOTAL	5	159.31	0.00	338.63	0.00	15.61	17,124.45	2,568,575.00	42,118.90	59,756.90
STATE TOTAL	40	14,089.78	0.00	24,952.65	0.00	1,182.72	241,875.36	25,376,299.10	952,009.46	1,234,089.97
SOUTH DAKOTA										
HURON WMD BEADLE	*	0.00	0.00	240.00	0.00	40.00	7,256.45	1,651,212.69	34,450.85	41,987.30
BUFFALO		0.00	0.00	0.00	0.00	0.00	0.00	0.00	1,523.61	1,523.61
HAND	*	80.00	0.00	0.00	0.00	79.00	3,671.31	580,260.35	46,857.65	50,687.96
HUGHES		0.00	0.00	0.00	0.00	0.00	455.99	82,800.00	744.50	1,200.49
HYDE	*	0.00	0.00	0.00	0.00	1,441.36	0.00	0.00	26,388.27	27,829.63
JERAULD	*	40.00	0.00	0.00	0.00	320.00	1,430.40	217,041.00	21,121.33	22,911.73
SANBORN	*	0.00	0.00	0.00	0.00	0.00	93.00	5,250.00	35,954.25	36,047.25
SULLY	*	0.00	0.00	0.00	0.00	0.00	266.48	9,993.00	3,809.51	4,075.99
WMD TOTAL	8	120.00	0.00	240.00	0.00	1,880.36	13,173.63	2,546,557.04	170,849.97	186,263.96
LACREEK WMD HAAKON FSA	** *	0.00	0.00	0.00	0.00	0.00	0.00	0.00	1,806.10	1,806.10
JONES FSA	** *	0.00	0.00	0.00	0.00	0.00	0.00	0.00	232.00	232.00
STANLEY FSA	** *	0.00	0.00	0.00	0.00	0.00	0.00	0.00	1,404.80	1,404.80
WMD TOTAL	0	0.00	0.00	0.00	0.00	0.00	0.00	0.00	3,442.90	3,442.90
LAKE ANDES WMD AURORA	*	0.00	0.00	0.00	0.00	0.00	4,716.08	622,316.00	29,796.38	34,512.46
BON HOMME	*	0.00	0.00	0.00	0.00	0.00	1,174.17	323,624.90	252.73	1,426.90
BRULE		0.00	0.00	0.00	0.00	0.00	1,074.13	89,404.00	17,566.69	18,640.82
CHARLES MIX	*	0.00	0.00	0.00	0.00	285.70	4,098.15	1,142,147.00	7,381.30	11,765.15
CLAY	*	0.00	0.00	0.00	0.00	0.00	40.00	8,000.00	59.50	99.50
DAVISON	*	0.00	0.00	0.00	0.00	0.00	229.92	24,540.00	354.10	584.02
DOUGLAS	*	0.00	0.00	0.00	0.00	449.73	3,852.05	647,691.00	3,450.61	7,752.39
HANSON	*	0.00	0.00	0.00	0.00	0.00	1,075.60	281,853.00	2,813.28	3,888.88
HUTCHINSON	*	0.00	0.00	0.00	0.00	0.00	789.51	227,646.25	1,185.50	1,975.01
LINCOLN		0.00	0.00	0.00	0.00	0.00	177.22	39,925.00	300.50	477.72
TRIPP FSA	** *	0.00	0.00	0.00	0.00	0.00	0.00	0.00	5.90	5.90
TURNER	*	0.00	0.00	0.00	0.00	0.00	850.09	430,044.90	479.90	1,329.99
UNION		0.00	0.00	0.00	0.00	0.00	96.02	22,331.00	0.00	96.02
YANKTON		0.00	0.00	0.00	0.00	0.00	294.63	128,562.00	346.50	641.13
WMD TOTAL	13	0.00	0.00	0.00	0.00	735.43	18,467.57	3,988,085.05	63,992.89	83,195.89

TABLE 4 - WATERFOWL PRODUCTION AREA COUNTIES

STATE AND UNIT		RESERVED FROM PUBLIC DOMAIN		ACQUIRED BY OTHER FEDERAL AGENCY		DEVISE OR GIFT	PURCHASED		AGREEMENT EASEMENT OR LEASE	TOTAL ACRES
		SOLE OR PRIMARY	SECONDARY	SOLE OR PRIMARY	SECONDARY		ACRES	COST ($)		
SOUTH DAKOTA										
MADISON WMD BROOKINGS	*	0.00	0.00	0.00	0.00	158.25	6,075.80	1,430,276.70	7,309.58	13,543.63
DEUEL	*	0.00	0.00	0.00	0.00	0.00	3,186.37	499,022.00	22,305.83	25,492.20
HAMLIN	*	0.00	0.00	0.00	0.00	0.00	3,400.89	954,563.00	6,319.14	9,720.03
KINGSBURY	*	0.00	0.00	0.00	0.00	0.00	6,924.04	1,838,689.80	23,806.78	30,730.82
LAKE	*	0.00	0.00	0.00	0.00	339.34	5,661.50	1,224,017.75	5,948.25	11,949.09
MCCOOK	*	0.00	0.00	0.00	0.00	0.00	3,362.96	680,845.60	7,129.37	10,492.33
MINER	*	40.00	0.00	0.00	0.00	0.00	1,537.04	151,040.00	19,533.92	21,110.96
MINNEHAHA	*	0.00	0.00	0.00	0.00	0.00	4,488.84	1,096,786.00	1,650.96	6,139.80
MOODY	*	0.00	0.00	0.00	0.00	277.22	2,903.78	927,478.85	1,203.67	4,384.67
WMD TOTAL	9	40.00	0.00	0.00	0.00	774.81	37,541.22	8,762,719.70	95,207.50	133,563.53
SAND LAKE WMD BROWN		0.00	0.00	0.00	0.00	482.62	4,094.93	819,223.80	48,524.67	53,102.22
CAMPBELL		240.00	0.00	0.00	0.00	0.00	1,919.71	185,541.00	21,272.71	23,432.42
CORSON FSA	** *	0.00	0.00	0.00	0.00	0.00	0.00	0.00	1,105.90	1,105.90
DEWEY FSA	** *	0.00	0.00	0.00	0.00	0.00	0.00	0.00	956.80	956.80
EDMUNDS	*	0.00	0.00	0.00	0.00	160.00	8,965.76	1,717,201.00	114,160.49	123,286.25
FAULK	*	0.00	0.00	0.00	0.00	0.00	2,566.88	480,995.00	124,936.62	127,503.50
MCPHERSON	*	160.45	0.00	0.00	0.00	1,381.23	19,402.37	3,397,500.80	134,466.16	155,410.21
POTTER	*	0.00	0.00	0.00	0.00	0.00	652.63	71,179.00	23,201.33	23,853.96
SPINK	*	520.00	0.00	0.00	0.00	200.00	2,226.43	388,680.00	25,234.55	28,180.98
WALWORTH	*	335.71	0.00	0.00	0.00	0.00	1,524.54	191,800.00	17,010.71	18,870.96
WMD TOTAL	8	1,256.16	0.00	0.00	0.00	2,223.85	41,353.25	7,252,120.60	510,869.94	555,703.20
WAUBAY WMD CLARK	*	95.75	0.00	0.00	0.00	0.00	6,053.11	843,303.90	44,686.02	50,814.86
CODINGTON	*	31.23	0.00	0.00	0.00	1,188.42	5,089.31	882,837.70	10,053.45	16,362.41
DAY		208.75	0.00	0.00	0.00	0.00	6,411.50	466,966.00	44,809.51	51,429.76
GRANT		0.00	0.00	0.00	0.00	0.00	5,362.99	1,005,000.00	15,254.87	20,617.86
MARSHALL	*	16.89	0.00	0.00	0.00	204.95	10,484.79	1,951,929.00	55,812.56	66,519.19
ROBERTS	*	0.00	0.00	0.00	0.00	0.00	5,032.73	625,710.80	50,762.48	55,795.21
WMD TOTAL	6	352.60	0.00	0.00	0.00	1,393.37	38,414.43	5,775,747.40	221,378.89	261,539.29
STATE TOTAL	44	1,768.76	0.00	240.00	0.00	7,007.82	148,950.10	28,325,229.79	1,065,742.09	1,223,708.77
WISCONSIN										
LEOPOLD WMD ADAMS		0.00	0.00	0.00	0.00	0.00	344.00	172,500.00	0.00	344.00
COLUMBIA		0.00	0.00	0.00	0.00	0.00	2,922.43	2,556,666.45	0.00	2,922.43
DANE		0.00	0.00	0.00	0.00	0.00	1,592.08	2,109,875.65	0.00	1,592.08
DODGE		0.00	0.00	0.00	0.00	0.00	855.41	812,371.16	.43	855.84
FOND DU LAC		0.00	0.00	0.00	0.00	0.00	833.95	915,452.00	0.00	833.95
JEFFERSON		0.00	0.00	0.00	0.00	0.00	249.79	241,239.00	0.00	249.79
MANITOWOC		0.00	0.00	0.00	0.00	0.00	120.00	88,000.00	0.00	120.00
MARQUETTE		0.00	0.00	0.00	0.00	0.00	259.97	119,480.00	0.00	259.97
OZAUKEE		0.00	0.00	0.00	0.00	0.00	536.30	679,415.40	0.00	536.30
ROCK		0.00	0.00	0.00	0.00	0.00	349.32	302,358.71	0.00	349.32
SHEBOYGAN		0.00	0.00	0.00	0.00	0.00	537.98	1,055,638.94	0.00	537.98
WAUSHARA		0.00	0.00	0.00	0.00	0.00	252.30	243,000.00	0.00	252.30
WINNEBAGO		0.00	0.00	0.00	0.00	0.00	1,918.27	1,331,300.00	0.00	1,918.27
WMD TOTAL	13	0.00	0.00	0.00	0.00	0.00	10,751.80	10,407,295.31	.43	10,752.23
ST. CROIX WMD DUNN		0.00	0.00	0.00	0.00	0.00	621.98	698,200.00	0.00	621.98
POLK		0.00	0.00	0.00	0.00	0.00	1,045.07	509,094.00	0.00	1,045.07

TABLE 4 - WATERFOWL PRODUCTION AREA COUNTIES

STATE AND UNIT		RESERVED FROM PUBLIC DOMAIN		ACQUIRED BY OTHER FEDERAL AGENCY		DEVISE OR GIFT	PURCHASED		AGREEMENT EASEMENT OR LEASE	TOTAL ACRES
		SOLE OR PRIMARY	SECONDARY	SOLE OR PRIMARY	SECONDARY		ACRES	COST ($)		
WISCONSIN										
ST. CROIX WMD										
ST. CROIX		0.00	0.00	0.00	0.00	0.00	5,091.90	5,356,004.56	1.00	5,092.90
WMD TOTAL	3	0.00	0.00	0.00	0.00	0.00	6,758.95	6,563,298.56	1.00	6,759.95
STATE TOTAL	16	0.00	0.00	0.00	0.00	0.00	17,510.75	16,970,593.87	1.43	17,512.18
GRAND TOTAL	203	15,897.64	0.00	26,766.89	0.00	11,768.32	681,127.29	187,198,559.07	2,204,030.28	2,939,590.42

*   - COUNTY WHERE WPA PROGRAM CURRENTLY EXISTS AND NEW FSA INTERESTS ARE ACQUIRED.

** *   - SUMMARY BY COUNTY OF ALL OTHER ACRES, BOTH FEE AND LESS THAN FEE, ACQUIRED FROM THE FSA, NOT REPORTED WITHIN AN EXISTING PROJECT. SUMMARY MAY CONTAIN ONE OR MORE OWNERSHIPS. FSA COUNTY SUMMARY ACRES ARE INCLUDED IN THE TOTAL ACRES FOR EACH STATE BUT ARE NOT SEPARATE UNITS IN THE WATERFOWL PRODUCTION AREA STATE TOTALS.

WMD   - WETLANDS MANAGEMENT DISTRICT

FSA   - FARM SERVICE AGENCY (FORMERLY FARMERS HOME ADMINISTRATION, DEPARTMENT OF AGRICULTURE)

TABLE 5 - COORDINATION AREAS

STATE AND UNIT	RESERVED FROM PUBLIC DOMAIN		ACQUIRED BY OTHER FEDERAL AGENCY		DEVISE OR GIFT	PURCHASED		AGREEMEN EASEMENT OR LEASE	TOTAL ACRES
	SOLE OR PRIMARY	SECONDARY	SOLE OR PRIMARY	SECONDARY		ACRES	COST ($)		
ARIZONA GILA RIVER	6,896.14	0.00	0.00	0.00	0.00	0.00	0.00	0.00	6,896.14
STATE TOTAL 1	6,896.14	0.00	0.00	0.00	0.00	0.00	0.00	0.00	6,896.14
CALIFORNIA HONEY LAKE	1,050.29	0.00	0.00	0.00	0.00	0.00	0.00	0.00	1,050.29
TOPAZ LAKE	200.00	0.00	0.00	0.00	0.00	0.00	0.00	0.00	200.00
STATE TOTAL 2	1,250.29	0.00	0.00	0.00	0.00	0.00	0.00	0.00	1,250.29
COLORADO HOT SULPHUR	1,115.00	0.00	0.00	0.00	0.00	0.00	0.00	0.00	1,115.00
MACK MESA	37.53	0.00	0.00	0.00	0.00	0.00	0.00	0.00	37.53
STATE TOTAL 2	1,152.53	0.00	0.00	0.00	0.00	0.00	0.00	0.00	1,152.53
IDAHO C. J. STRIKE	1,544.90	0.00	0.00	0.00	0.00	0.00	0.00	0.00	1,544.90
CAREY LAKE	320.00	0.00	0.00	0.00	0.00	0.00	0.00	0.00	320.00
HAGERMAN	0.00	0.00	0.00	0.00	0.00	219.78	13,070.00	0.00	219.78
NORTH LAKE	2,705.32	0.00	0.00	0.00	0.00	0.00	0.00	0.00	2,705.32
SAND CREEK	1,000.00	0.00	0.00	0.00	0.00	0.00	0.00	0.00	1,000.00
STATE TOTAL 5	5,570.22	0.00	0.00	0.00	0.00	219.78	13,070.00	0.00	5,790.00
ILLINOIS MISSISSIPPI RIVER	0.00	0.00	0.00	E 26,626.00	0.00	0.00	0.00	0.00	26,626.00
STATE TOTAL 1	0.00	0.00	0.00	26,626.00	0.00	0.00	0.00	0.00	26,626.00
IOWA GREEN ISLAND	0.00	0.00	0.00 E	2,571.00	0.00	82.00	410.00	0.00	2,653.00
LAKE ODESSA	0.00	0.00	0.00 E	3,134.00	0.00	0.00	0.00	0.00	3,134.00
PRINCETON	0.00	0.00	0.00 E	794.00	0.00	0.00	0.00	0.00	794.00
STATE TOTAL 3	0.00	0.00	0.00	6,499.00	0.00	82.00	410.00	0.00	6,581.00
MINNESOTA BELTRAMI	0.00	0.00	81,720.88	0.00	0.00	0.00	0.00	0.00	81,720.88
PIPESTONE	0.00	0.00	117.72	0.00	0.00	0.00	0.00	0.00	117.72
STATE TOTAL 2	0.00	0.00	81,858.60	0.00	0.00	0.00	0.00	0.00	81,858.60
MISSOURI CLARKSVILLE	0.00	0.00	0.00 E	282.00	0.00	0.00	0.00	0.00	282.00
ELSBERRY	0.00	0.00	0.00 E	1,786.00	0.00	0.00	0.00	0.00	1,286.00
MISSISSIPPI RIVER	0.00	0.00	0.00 E	10,265.00	0.00	0.00	0.00	0.00	10,265.00
WEST QUINCY	0.00	0.00	0.00 E	242.00	0.00	0.00	0.00	0.00	242.00
STATE TOTAL 4	0.00	0.00	0.00	12,075.00	0.00	0.00	0.00	0.00	12,075.00
MONTANA BULL MOUNTAIN	1,599.32	0.00	0.00	0.00	0.00	0.00	0.00	0.00	1,599.32
DODSON	120.00	0.00	0.00	0.00	0.00	0.00	0.00	0.00	120.00
FOX LAKE	160.00	0.00	0.00	0.00	0.00	0.00	0.00	0.00	160.00
FREEZEOUT LAKE	434.80	0.00	0.00	0.00	0.00	0.00	0.00	0.00	434.80
JUDITH RIVER	234.49	0.00	0.00	0.00	0.00	0.00	0.00	0.00	234.49
SUN RIVER	4,144.83	0.00	0.00	0.00	0.00	0.00	0.00	0.00	4,144.83
STATE TOTAL 6	6,693.44	0.00	0.00	0.00	0.00	0.00	0.00	0.00	6,693.44
NEVADA STILLWATER	0.00	0.00	0.00	0.00	0.00	0.00	0.00	63,544.00	63,544.00
STATE TOTAL 1	0.00	0.00	0.00	0.00	0.00	0.00	0.00	63,544.00	63,544.00

TABLE 5 — COORDINATION AREAS

STATE AND UNIT	RESERVED FROM PUBLIC DOMAIN		ACQUIRED BY OTHER FEDERAL AGENCY		DEVISE OR GIFT	PURCHASED		AGREEMENT EASEMENT OR LEASE	TOTAL ACRES
	SOLE OR PRIMARY	SECONDARY	SOLE OR PRIMARY	SECONDARY		ACRES	COST ($)		
NEW YORK LIDO BEACH	0.00	0.00	22.42	0.00	0.00	0.00	0.00	0.00	22.42
STATE TOTAL 1	0.00	0.00	22.42	0.00	0.00	0.00	0.00	0.00	22.42
NORTH DAKOTA LAKE WASHINGTON	3.68	0.00	0.00	0.00	0.00	0.00	0.00	0.00	3.68
STATE TOTAL 1	3.68	0.00	0.00	0.00	0.00	0.00	0.00	0.00	3.68
OREGON GOVERNMENT ISLAND	1.79	0.00	0.00	0.00	0.00	0.00	0.00	0.00	1.79
OCHOCO RESERVOIR	40.00	0.00	0.00	0.00	0.00	0.00	0.00	0.00	40.00
SUMMER LAKE	7,127.65	0.00	0.00	0.00	0.00	0.00	0.00	0.00	7,127.65
STATE TOTAL 3	7,169.44	0.00	0.00	0.00	0.00	0.00	0.00	0.00	7,169.44
UTAH DESERT LAKES	880.00	0.00	1,741.23	0.00	0.00	0.00	0.00	0.00	2,621.23
ROCK ISLAND	1.74	0.00	0.00	0.00	0.00	0.00	0.00	0.00	1.74
TOPAZ LAKE	3,662.13	0.00	480.00	0.00	0.00	0.00	0.00	0.00	4,142.13
STATE TOTAL 3	4,543.87	0.00	2,221.23	0.00	0.00	0.00	0.00	0.00	6,765.10
WASHINGTON COLOCKUM	4,957.23	0.00	0.00	0.00	0.00	0.00	0.00	0.00	4,957.23
LENORE	5,787.00	0.00	0.00	0.00	0.00	0.00	0.00	0.00	5,787.00
HARROWSTONE	16.25	0.00	0.00	0.00	0.00	0.00	0.00	0.00	16.25
METHOW	3,037.97	0.00	0.00	0.00	0.00	0.00	0.00	0.00	3,037.97
PHALON LAKE	9.70	0.00	0.00	0.00	0.00	0.00	0.00	0.00	9.70
SHERMAN CREEK	560.00	0.00	0.00	0.00	0.00	0.00	0.00	0.00	560.00
SINLAHEKIN	2,833.83	0.00	0.00	0.00	0.00	0.00	0.00	0.00	2,833.83
SUNNYSIDE	320.00	0.00	0.00	0.00	0.00	0.00	0.00	0.00	320.00
STATE TOTAL 8	17,521.98	0.00	0.00	0.00	0.00	0.00	0.00	0.00	17,521.98
WISCONSIN NECEDAH	33.18	0.00	55,260.72	0.00	0.00	379.35	0.00	0.00	55,673.25
STATE TOTAL 1	33.18	0.00	55,260.72	0.00	0.00	379.35	0.00	0.00	55,673.25
WYOMING EAST FORK	3,432.04	0.00	0.00	0.00	0.00	0.00	0.00	0.00	3,432.04
GREYS RIVER	927.31	0.00	0.00	0.00	0.00	0.00	0.00	0.00	927.31
OCEAN LAKE	0.00	0.00	0.00 R	10,539.14	0.00	0.00	0.00	0.00	10,539.14
SHERIDAN	160.00	0.00	0.00	0.00	0.00	0.00	0.00	0.00	160.00
SYBILLE	681.44	0.00	0.00	0.00	0.00	0.00	0.00	0.00	681.44
TONGUE RIVER	551.05	0.00	0.00	0.00	0.00	0.00	0.00	0.00	551.05
STATE TOTAL 6	5,751.84	0.00	0.00	10,539.14	0.00	0.00	0.00	0.00	16,290.98
GRAND TOTAL 50	56,586.61	0.00	139,342.97	55,739.14	0.00	681.13	15,480.00	65,544.00	315,893.85

E — CORPS OF ENGINEERS — DEPARTMENT OF THE ARMY
R. — BUREAU OF RECLAMATION — DEPARTMENT OF THE INTERIOR

TABLE 6 - ADMINISTRATIVE SITES

STATE AND UNIT	RESERVED FROM PUBLIC DOMAIN		ACQUIRED BY OTHER FEDERAL AGENCY		DEVISE OR GIFT	PURCHASED		AGREEMENT EASEMENT OR LEASE	TOTAL ACRES
	SOLE OR PRIMARY	SECONDARY	SOLE OR PRIMARY	SECONDARY		ACRES	COST ($)		
ALASKA									
BETHEL	5.08	0.00	0.00	0.00	0.00	2.08	63,600.00	0.00	7.16
BETTLES	0.00	0.00	0.00	0.00	0.00	0.00	0.00	1.74	1.74
COLD BAY HANGAR	0.00	0.00	0.00	0.00	0.00	0.00	0.00	.39	.39
DILLINGHAM	0.00	0.00	0.00	0.00	0.00	13.73	499,900.00	0.00	13.73
EMMONAK	0.00	0.00	0.00	0.00	0.00	0.00	0.00	.17	.17
FAIRBANKS HANGAR	0.00	0.00	0.00	0.00	0.00	0.00	0.00	2.04	2.04
FAIRBANKS OFFICE WILDLIFE	0.00	0.00	1.89	0.00	0.00	.26	2,024.05	0.00	2.15
FAIRBANKS WAREHOUSE	.64	0.00	0.00	0.00	0.00	0.00	0.00	0.00	.64
FORT YUKON	.52	0.00	0.00	0.00	0.00	0.00	0.00	.19	.71
GALENA	.44	0.00	0.00	0.00	0.00	2.99	50,100.00	0.00	3.43
HOMER	0.00	0.00	0.00	0.00	.75	57.80	1,009,000.00	0.00	58.55
JUNEAU DOCK	0.00	0.00	0.00	0.00	0.00	0.00	0.00	.67	.67
JUNEAU HANGAR	0.00	0.00	0.00	0.00	0.00	0.00	0.00	1.06	1.06
KAKTOVIK	0.00	0.00	0.00	0.00	0.00	0.00	0.00	.46	.46
KENAI HANGAR	0.00	0.00	0.00	0.00	0.00	0.00	0.00	.91	.91
KETCHIKAN	0.00	0.00	0.00	0.00	0.00	0.00	0.00	.31	.31
KING SALMON	6.29	0.00	0.00	0.00	0.00	5.42	64,800.00	0.00	11.71
KODIAK	2.04	0.00	0.00	0.00	0.00	0.00	0.00	0.00	2.04
KODIAK FLOAT PLANE	0.00	0.00	0.00	0.00	0.00	0.00	0.00	.06	.06
KODIAK OFFICE	0.00	0.00	0.00	0.00	36.00	0.00	0.00	0.00	36.00
KOTZEBUE	0.00	0.00	0.00	0.00	0.00	.50	209,500.00	0.00	.50
KUSTATAN RIVER	0.00	0.00	0.00	0.00	0.00	0.00	0.00	7.00	7.00
LAKE HOOD SEAPLANE BASE	14.90	0.00	0.00	0.00	0.00	0.00	0.00	2.26	17.16
LEWIS RIVER	0.00	0.00	0.00	0.00	0.00	0.00	0.00	6.00	6.00
MCGRATH	0.00	0.00	0.00	0.00	0.00	2.44	51,000.00	0.00	2.44
MCLEES LAKE	0.00	0.00	0.00	0.00	0.00	0.00	0.00	.01	.01
MORTENSENS CREEK	0.00	0.00	0.00	0.00	0.00	0.00	0.00	1.50	1.50
PILOT POINT	0.00	0.00	0.00	0.00	0.00	0.00	0.00	5.00	5.00
SOLDOTNA AIRPORT	0.00	0.00	0.00	0.00	0.00	0.00	0.00	3.92	3.92
ST. GEORGE	0.00	0.00	0.00	0.00	0.00	0.00	0.00	1.00	1.00
ST. PAUL	0.00	0.00	0.00	0.00	0.00	0.00	0.00	1.11	1.11
TOK	0.00	0.00	0.00	0.00	0.00	17.88	45,000.00	0.00	17.88
WHITEFISH LAKE	0.00	0.00	0.00	0.00	0.00	0.00	0.00	.50	.50
STATE TOTAL 33	29.91	0.00	1.89	0.00	36.75	103.10	1,994,924.05	36.30	207.95
ARIZONA									
CABEZA PRIETA	10.00	0.00	0.00	0.00	0.00	.44	25,300.00	0.00	10.44
KOFA	0.00	0.00	0.00	0.00	0.00	1.00	2.00	0.00	1.00
STATE TOTAL 2	10.00	0.00	0.00	0.00	0.00	1.44	25,302.00	0.00	11.44
CALIFORNIA									
SAN SIMEON (B) *	0.00	0.00	0.00	0.00	0.00	0.00	0.00	0.00	0.00
STATE TOTAL 0	0.00	0.00	0.00	0.00	0.00	0.00	0.00	0.00	0.00
COLORADO									
NAT'L BLACK-FOOTED FERRET	0.00	0.00	0.00	0.00	0.00	40.05	32,000.00	0.00	40.05
STATE TOTAL 1	0.00	0.00	0.00	0.00	0.00	40.05	32,000.00	0.00	40.05
HAWAII									
HAWAII	0.00	0.00	.23	0.00	0.00	0.00	0.00	0.00	.23
MAKENA BEACH	0.00	0.00	0.00	0.00	0.00	0.00	0.00	.50	.50
OLINDA	0.00	0.00	4.20	0.00	0.00	0.00	0.00	0.00	4.20
STATE TOTAL 3	0.00	0.00	4.43	0.00	0.00	0.00	0.00	.50	4.93

TABLE 6 — ADMINISTRATIVE SITES

STATE AND UNIT	RESERVED FROM PUBLIC DOMAIN		ACQUIRED BY OTHER FEDERAL AGENCY		DEVISE OR GIFT	PURCHASED		AGREEMENT EASEMENT OR LEASE	TOTAL ACRES
	SOLE OR PRIMARY	SECONDARY	SOLE OR PRIMARY	SECONDARY		ACRES	COST ($)		
IOWA MCGREGOR	0.00	0.00	0.00	0.00	0.00	4.33	155,000.00	0.00	4.33
STATE TOTAL 1	0.00	0.00	0.00	0.00	0.00	4.33	155,000.00	0.00	4.33
KANSAS GREAT PLAINS NATURE CTR	0.00	0.00	0.00	0.00	0.00	8.33	400,000.00	6.22	14.55
STATE TOTAL 1	0.00	0.00	0.00	0.00	0.00	8.33	400,000.00	6.22	14.55
MICHIGAN LAMPREY EEL	0.00	0.00	0.00	0.00	0.00	0.00	0.00	1.00	1.00
STATE TOTAL 1	0.00	0.00	0.00	0.00	0.00	0.00	0.00	1.00	1.00
NEW MEXICO SAN ANDRES	0.00	0.00	0.00	0.00	0.00	2.16	14,000.00	0.00	2.16
STATE TOTAL 1	0.00	0.00	0.00	0.00	0.00	2.16	14,000.00	0.00	2.16
OREGON CLARK R. BAVIN (A)	0.00	0.00	0.00	0.00	0.00	0.00	0.00	4.02	4.02
KLAMATH	10.04	0.00	0.00	0.00	0.00	0.00	0.00	0.00	10.04
LAKEVIEW	0.00	0.00	.25	0.00	0.00	0.00	0.00	0.00	.25
STATE TOTAL 3	10.04	0.00	.25	0.00	0.00	0.00	0.00	4.02	14.31
WASHINGTON MOSES LAKE	0.00	0.00	.83	0.00	0.00	0.00	0.00	0.00	.83
STATE TOTAL 1	0.00	0.00	.83	0.00	0.00	0.00	0.00	0.00	.83
WEST VIRGINIA NCTC/TRAINING CENTER	0.00	0.00	0.00	0.00	0.00	865.74	7,949,045.00	0.00	865.74
STATE TOTAL 1	0.00	0.00	0.00	0.00	0.00	865.74	7,949,045.00	0.00	865.74
GRAND TOTAL 48	49.95	0.00	7.40	0.00	36.75	1,025.15	10,570,271.05	48.04	1,167.29

(A) — FISH AND WILDLIFE FORENSICS LAB
(B) — OPERATED BY USGS/BRD
* — NOT COUNTED

TABLE 7 - NATIONAL FISH HATCHERIES

STATE AND UNIT	RESERVED FROM PUBLIC DOMAIN		ACQUIRED BY OTHER FEDERAL AGENCY		DEVISE OR GIFT	PURCHASED		AGREEMENT EASEMENT OR LEASE	TOTAL ACRES
	SOLE OR PRIMARY	SECONDARY	SOLE OR PRIMARY	SECONDARY		ACRES	COST ($)		
ARIZONA									
ALCHESAY	0.00	0.00	0.00	0.00	0.00	0.00	0.00	20.83	20.83
WILLIAMS CREEK	0.00	0.00	0.00	0.00	0.00	0.00	0.00	91.89	91.89
WILLOW BEACH	0.00	R 47.81	0.00	0.00	0.00	0.00	0.00	0.00	47.81
STATE TOTAL 3	0.00	47.81	0.00	0.00	0.00	0.00	0.00	112.72	160.55
ARKANSAS									
GREERS FERRY	0.00	0.00	0.00	E 31.97	0.00	0.00	0.00	0.00	31.97
MAMMOTH SPRING	0.00	0.00	0.00	0.00	0.00	36.84	55,925.00	0.00	36.84
NORFORK	0.00	0.00	0.00	E 46.00	0.00	0.00	0.00	0.00	46.00
STATE TOTAL 3	0.00	0.00	0.00	77.97	0.00	36.84	55,925.00	0.00	114.81
CALIFORNIA									
COLEMAN	0.00	0.00	55.28	0.00	0.00	22.52	153,221.00	62.97	140.77
LIVINGSTON STONE	0.00	0.00	0.00	0.00	0.00	0.00	0.00	.04	.04
TEHAMA-COLUSA (D) *	0.00	0.00	0.00	R 350.00	0.00	0.00	0.00	0.00	350.00
STATE TOTAL 2	0.00	0.00	55.28	350.00	0.00	22.52	153,221.00	63.01	490.81
COLORADO									
HOTCHKISS	10.00	0.00	129.17	0.00	0.00	0.00	0.00	2.54	141.71
LEADVILLE	2,966.34	0.00	0.00	0.00	0.00	98.79	14,400.00	.75	3,065.88
STATE TOTAL 2	2,976.34	0.00	129.17	0.00	0.00	98.79	14,400.00	3.29	3,207.59
FLORIDA									
WELAKA	0.00	0.00	385.04	0.00	0.00	0.00	0.00	0.00	385.04
STATE TOTAL 1	0.00	0.00	385.04	0.00	0.00	0.00	0.00	0.00	385.04
GEORGIA									
BO GINN (A) *	0.00	0.00	0.00	0.00	106.89	20.12	10.00	0.00	127.01
CHATTAHOOCHEE FOREST	0.00	0.00	0.00	F 44.80	0.00	0.00	0.00	0.00	44.80
WARM SPRINGS (H)	0.00	0.00	0.00	0.00	18.97	37.24	24,916.00	0.00	56.21
STATE TOTAL 2	0.00	0.00	0.00	44.80	125.86	57.36	24,926.00	0.00	228.02
IDAHO									
CLEARWATER FISH HATCHERY (A) *	0.00	0.00	17.62	0.00	0.00	0.00	0.00	1.33	18.95
DWORSHAK	0.00	0.00	0.00	0.00	0.00	0.00	0.00	23.54	23.54
EAGLE FISH (I) *	0.00	0.00	1.21	0.00	0.00	0.00	0.00	.18	1.39
HAGERMAN	0.00	0.00	0.00	0.00	0.00	78.79	4,566.22	0.00	78.79
KOOSKIA	125.20	0.00	0.00	0.00	0.00	3.25	1.00	8.99	137.44
MAGIC VALLEY (A) *	0.00	0.00	25.46	0.00	0.00	0.00	0.00	16.98	42.44
MCCALL (A) *	0.00	0.00	10.91	0.00	0.00	0.00	0.00	19.05	29.96
SAWTOOTH (A) *	0.00	0.00	71.66	0.00	0.00	0.00	0.00	11.63	83.29
STATE TOTAL 3	125.20	0.00	126.86	0.00	0.00	82.04	4,567.22	81.70	415.80
KENTUCKY									
WOLF CREEK	0.00	0.00	0.00	E 20.47	0.00	0.00	0.00	0.00	20.47
STATE TOTAL 1	0.00	0.00	0.00	20.47	0.00	0.00	0.00	0.00	20.47
LOUISIANA									
NATCHITOCHES	0.00	0.00	0.00	0.00	0.00	96.99	3,954.95	0.00	96.99
STATE TOTAL 1	0.00	0.00	0.00	0.00	0.00	96.99	3,954.95	0.00	96.99

TABLE 7 - NATIONAL FISH HATCHERIES

STATE AND UNIT		RESERVED FROM PUBLIC DOMAIN		ACQUIRED BY OTHER FEDERAL AGENCY		DEVISE OR GIFT	PURCHASED		AGREEMENT EASEMENT OR LEASE	TOTAL ACRES
		SOLE OR PRIMARY	SECONDARY	SOLE OR PRIMARY	SECONDARY		ACRES	COST ($)		
MAINE										
CRAIG BROOK		0.00	0.00	0.00	0.00	0.00	134.65	2,000.00	0.00	134.65
GREEN LAKE		0.00	0.00	0.00	0.00	0.00	128.86	32,000.00	1.00	129.86
STATE TOTAL	2	0.00	0.00	0.00	0.00	0.00	263.51	34,000.00	1.00	264.51
MASSACHUSETTS										
BERKSHIRE	(A) *	0.00	0.00	0.00	0.00	136.90	0.00	2,500.00	0.00	136.90
NORTH ATTLEBORO		0.00	0.00	0.00	0.00	228.48	.06	1,500.00	0.00	228.54
RICHARD CRONIN		0.00	0.00	0.00	0.00	59.69	0.00	0.00	0.00	59.69
STATE TOTAL	2	0.00	0.00	0.00	0.00	425.07	.06	4,000.00	0.00	425.13
MICHIGAN										
HIAWATHA FOREST		0.00	0.00	0.00	6.67	0.00	0.00	0.00	0.00	6.67
JORDAN RIVER		0.00	0.00	0.00	0.00	116.84	0.00	0.00	0.00	116.84
PENDILLS CREEK		0.00	0.00	0.00 F	1,646.65	0.00	84.81	4,000.00	0.00	1,731.46
STATE TOTAL	3	0.00	0.00	0.00	1,653.32	116.84	84.81	4,000.00	0.00	1,854.97
MISSISSIPPI										
MERIDIAN	(A) *	0.00	0.00	0.00	0.00	105.86	0.00	0.00	0.00	105.86
PRIVATE JOHN ALLEN		0.00	0.00	0.00	0.00	0.00	28.40	1,990.00	0.00	28.40
STATE TOTAL	1	0.00	0.00	0.00	0.00	105.86	28.40	1,990.00	0.00	134.26
MISSOURI										
NEOSHO		0.00	0.00	0.00	0.00	0.00	261.33	46,027.97	11.50	272.83
STATE TOTAL	1	0.00	0.00	0.00	0.00	0.00	261.33	46,027.97	11.50	272.83
MONTANA										
BOZEMAN	(F) *	0.00	0.00	0.00	0.00	42.79	130.30	4,565.00	.28	173.37
CRESTON		0.00	0.00	73.56	0.00	0.00	0.00	0.00	0.00	73.56
ENNIS		0.00	0.00	0.00	0.00	0.00	160.00	4,000.00	9.32	169.32
STATE TOTAL	2	0.00	0.00	73.56	0.00	42.79	290.30	8,565.00	9.60	416.25
NEVADA										
ARMAGOSA PUPFISH	(D) *	0.00	LM 159.28	0.00	0.00	0.00	0.00	0.00	0.00	159.28
LAHONTAN		0.00	0.00	0.00	0.00	0.00	24.84	12,200.00	11.06	35.90
MARBLE BLUFF	(D) *	0.00	0.00	0.00 R	623.20	0.00	0.00	0.00	0.00	623.20
STATE TOTAL	1	0.00	159.28	0.00	623.20	0.00	24.84	12,200.00	11.06	818.38
NEW HAMPSHIRE										
MERRIMACK RIVER	(C) *	0.00	0.00	0.00	0.00	0.00	8.00	24,000.00	0.00	8.00
NASHUA		0.00	0.00	0.00	0.00	0.00	39.40	4,000.00	0.00	39.40
STATE TOTAL	1	0.00	0.00	0.00	0.00	0.00	47.40	28,000.00	0.00	47.40
NEW MEXICO										
DEXTER	(G)	0.00	0.00	0.00	0.00	0.00	640.00	3,265.90	.93	640.93
MORA	(G)	0.00	0.00	0.00	0.00	0.00	116.79	241,000.00	2.00	118.79
STATE TOTAL	2	0.00	0.00	0.00	0.00	0.00	756.79	244,265.90	2.93	759.72
NORTH CAROLINA										
EDENTON		0.00	0.00	0.00	0.00	0.00	65.59	30,000.00	0.00	65.59
MCKINNEY LAKE	(A) *	0.00	0.00	408.07	0.00	0.00	14.20	72,000.00	0.00	422.27
STATE TOTAL	1	0.00	0.00	408.07	0.00	0.00	77.79	102,000.00	0.00	485.86

TABLE 7 - NATIONAL FISH HATCHERIES

STATE AND UNIT	RESERVED FROM PUBLIC DOMAIN		ACQUIRED BY OTHER FEDERAL AGENCY		DEVISE OR GIFT	PURCHASED		AGREEMENT EASEMENT OR LEASE	TOTAL ACRES
	SOLE OR PRIMARY	SECONDARY	SOLE OR PRIMARY	SECONDARY		ACRES	COST ($)		
NORTH DAKOTA									
BALDHILL DAM (D) *	0.00	0.00	0.00	E 37.10	0.00	0.00	0.00	0.00	37.10
GARRISON DAM	0.00	0.00	0.00	E 186.40	0.00	0.00	0.00	0.00	186.40
VALLEY CITY	0.00	0.00	0.00	0.00	71.49	0.00	0.00	.93	72.42
STATE TOTAL 2	0.00	0.00	0.00	223.50	71.49	0.00	0.00	.93	295.92
OKLAHOMA									
TISHOMINGO	0.00	0.00	0.00	0.00	0.00	230.95	99,157.00	3,428.55	3,659.50
STATE TOTAL 1	0.00	0.00	0.00	0.00	0.00	230.95	99,157.00	3,428.55	3,659.50
OREGON									
EAGLE CREEK	40.00	LM 560.00	0.00	0.00	0.00	126.37	17,000.00	1.03	727.40
IRRIGON SATELLITES (A) *	0.00	0.00	18.14	0.00	0.00	0.00	0.00	1.27	19.41
LOOKINGGLASS (A) *	0.00	0.00	13.49	0.00	0.00	0.00	0.00	0.00	13.49
WARM SPRINGS	0.00	0.00	0.00	0.00	0.00	0.00	0.00	84.79	84.79
STATE TOTAL 2	40.00	560.00	31.63	0.00	0.00	126.37	17,000.00	87.09	845.09
PENNSYLVANIA									
ALLEGHENY	0.00	0.00	0.00	E 45.04	0.00	0.00	0.00	0.00	45.04
LAHAR (H)	0.00	0.00	0.00	0.00	0.00	177.21	30,957.31	0.00	177.21
STATE TOTAL 2	0.00	0.00	0.00	45.04	0.00	177.21	30,957.31	0.00	222.25
SOUTH CAROLINA									
BEARS BLUFF	0.00	0.00	30.40	0.00	0.00	0.00	0.00	0.00	30.40
ORANGEBURG	0.00	0.00	0.00	0.00	0.00	50.65	6,578.40	0.00	50.65
ORANGEBURG COUNTY (D) *	0.00	0.00	0.00	0.00	134.01	46.65	7,500.00	0.00	180.66
STATE TOTAL 2	0.00	0.00	30.40	0.00	134.01	97.30	14,078.40	0.00	261.71
SOUTH DAKOTA									
D.C. BOOTH (E) *	0.00	0.00	0.00	0.00	0.00	10.67	4,100.00	.12	10.79
GAVINS POINT	0.00	0.00	0.00	E 581.00	0.00	0.00	0.00	0.00	581.00
STATE TOTAL 1	0.00	0.00	0.00	581.00	0.00	10.67	4,100.00	.12	591.79
TENNESSEE									
DALE HOLLOW	0.00	0.00	0.00	E 38.51	0.00	0.00	0.00	0.00	38.51
ERWIN	0.00	0.00	0.00	0.00	0.00	32.25	2,693.34	0.00	32.25
STATE TOTAL 2	0.00	0.00	0.00	38.51	0.00	32.25	2,693.34	0.00	70.76
TEXAS									
INKS DAM	0.00	0.00	0.00	0.00	84.70	0.00	0.00	89.20	173.90
SAN MARCOS (G)	0.00	0.00	0.00	0.00	115.78	0.00	0.00	2.79	118.57
UVALDE	0.00	0.00	0.00	0.00	100.00	0.00	0.00	1.06	101.06
STATE TOTAL 3	0.00	0.00	0.00	0.00	300.48	0.00	0.00	93.05	393.53
UTAH									
JONES HOLE	465.55	0.00	0.00	0.00	0.00	0.00	0.00	66.30	531.85
OURAY (3)	0.00	0.00	0.00	0.00	0.00	0.00	0.00	0.00	0.00
STATE TOTAL 2	465.55	0.00	0.00	0.00	0.00	0.00	0.00	66.30	531.85
VERMONT									
PITTSFORD	0.00	0.00	0.00	0.00	0.00	35.09	13,010.00	0.00	35.09
WHITE RIVER	0.00	0.00	0.00	0.00	0.00	53.50	133,320.00	15.00	68.50

TABLE 7 - NATIONAL FISH HATCHERIES

STATE AND UNIT	RESERVED FROM PUBLIC DOMAIN		ACQUIRED BY OTHER FEDERAL AGENCY		DEVISE OR GIFT	PURCHASED		AGREEMENT EASEMENT OR LEASE	TOTAL ACRES
	SOLE OR PRIMARY	SECONDARY	SOLE OR PRIMARY	SECONDARY		ACRES	COST ($)		
VERMONT									
STATE TOTAL 2	0.00	0.00	0.00	0.00	0.00	88.59	146,330.00	15.00	103.59
VIRGINIA									
HARRISON LAKE	0.00	0.00	0.00	0.00	0.00	444.73	116,368.50	0.00	444.73
PAINT BANK (A) *	0.00	0.00	0.00	0.00	0.00	0.00	51,500.00	0.00	0.00
WYTHEVILLE (A) *	0.00	0.00	0.00	0.00	0.00	(.00)	52,000.00	0.00	(.00)
STATE TOTAL 1	0.00	0.00	0.00	0.00	0.00	444.73	219,868.50	0.00	444.73
WASHINGTON									
ABERNATHY (C) *	0.00	0.00	0.00	0.00	0.00	98.52	10,789.00	3.10	101.62
CARSON	0.00	F 220.00	0.00	0.00	0.00	0.00	0.00	0.00	220.00
ENTIAT	0.00	0.00	34.27	0.00	0.00	0.00	0.00	.08	34.35
LEAVENWORTH	0.00	0.00	861.15	0.00	11.40	4.07	84,000.00	.43	877.05
LITTLE WHITE SALMON	0.00	0.00	211.39	0.00	0.00	203.78	474,563.00	17.42	432.59
LYONS FERRY (A) *	0.00	0.00	110.28	0.00	0.00	0.00	0.00	28.61	138.89
MAKAH	0.00	0.00	0.00	0.00	0.00	0.00	0.00	81.85	81.85
NISQUALLY (B) *	0.00	0.00	0.00	0.00	0.00	0.00	0.00	155.81	155.81
QUILCENE	0.00	0.00	0.00	0.00	3.38	29.36	341,530.00	12.52	45.26
QUINAULT	0.00	0.00	81.37	0.00	0.00	0.00	6,510.00	15.06	96.43
SPRING CREEK	0.00	0.00	0.00	E 24.20	0.00	55.70	87,475.00	9.67	89.57
TUCANNON (A) *	0.00	0.00	16.82	0.00	0.00	0.00	0.00	32.10	48.92
WILLARD	0.00	0.00	0.00	0.00	0.00	80.10	6,750.00	3.70	83.80
WINTHROP	0.00	0.00	41.56	0.00	0.00	0.00	0.00	12.37	53.93
STATE TOTAL 10	0.00	220.00	1,356.84	24.20	14.78	471.53	1,011,617.00	372.72	2,460.07
WEST VIRGINIA									
WHITE SULPHUR SPRINGS	0.00	0.00	0.00	0.00	0.00	23.24	2,500.00	0.00	23.24
STATE TOTAL 1	0.00	0.00	0.00	0.00	0.00	23.24	2,500.00	0.00	23.24
WISCONSIN									
GENOA (1)	0.00	0.00	0.00	0.00	0.00	0.00	0.00	0.00	0.00
IRON RIVER	0.00	0.00	0.00	0.00	0.00	880.83	285,480.00	0.00	880.83
STATE TOTAL 2	0.00	0.00	0.00	0.00	0.00	880.83	285,480.00	0.00	880.83
WYOMING									
JACKSON (2)	0.00	0.00	0.00	0.00	0.00	0.00	0.00	0.00	0.00
SARATOGA	0.00	0.00	0.00	0.00	0.00	118.73	174,800.00	1.21	119.94
STATE TOTAL 2	0.00	0.00	0.00	0.00	0.00	118.73	174,800.00	1.21	119.94
GRAND TOTAL 69	3,607.09	987.09	2,596.85	3,682.01	1,337.18	4,932.17	2,750,204.59	4,361.78	21,504.17

(A) — HATCHERY MANAGED/OPERATED BY STATE
(B) — HATCHERY MANAGED/OPERATED BY TRIBE
(C) — FISH TECHNOLOGY CENTER
(D) — OTHER NON-NATIONAL FISH HATCHERY OR FISHERIES FACILITY
(E) — HISTORIC NATIONAL FISH HATCHERY
(F) — FISH TECHNOLOGY AND FISH HEALTH CENTER
(G) — NATIONAL HATCHERY AND FISH TECHNOLOGY CENTER
(H) — NATIONAL FISH HATCHERY, FISH TECHNOLOGY CENTER AND FISH HEALTH CENTER
(I) — FISH HEALTH LAB MANAGED/OPERATED BY STATE

(1) — LOCATED ON THE UPPER MISSISSIPPI REFUGE
(2) — LOCATED ON THE NATIONAL ELK REFUGE
(3) — LOCATED ON THE OURAY NATIONAL WILDLIFE REFUGE

E — CORPS OF ENGINEERS, DEPARTMENT OF THE ARMY
F — FOREST SERVICE, DEPARTMENT OF AGRICULTURE
LM — BUREAU OF LAND MANAGEMENT, DEPARTMENT OF THE INTERIOR
R — BUREAU OF RECLAMATION, DEPARTMENT OF THE INTERIOR

* — NOT COUNTED AS A NATIONAL FISH HATCHERY

STATE AND UNIT	WILDERNESS NAME	WILDERNESS ACRES	REFUGE ACRES	PUBLIC LAW NUMBER	PUBLIC LAW DATE
ALASKA					
ALASKA MARITIME	ALEUTIAN ISLANDS	1,300,000.00	3,465,246.79	96-487	12-02-80
ALASKA MARITIME	BERING SEA	81,340.00	0.00	91-504	10-23-70
ALASKA MARITIME	BOGOSLOF	175.00	0.00	91-504	10-23-70
ALASKA MARITIME	CHAMISSO	455.00	0.00	93-632	01-03-75
ALASKA MARITIME	FORRESTER ISLAND	2,832.00	0.00	91-504	10-23-70
ALASKA MARITIME	HAZY ISLAND	32.00	0.00	91-504	10-23-70
ALASKA MARITIME	SEMIDI	250,000.00	0.00	96-487	12-02-80
ALASKA MARITIME	SIMEONOF	25,855.00	0.00	94-557	10-19-76
ALASKA MARITIME	ST. LAZARIA	65.00	0.00	91-504	10-23-70
ALASKA MARITIME	TUXEDNI	5,566.00	0.00	91-504	10-23-70
ALASKA MARITIME	UNIMAK	910,000.00	0.00	96-487	12-02-80
ARCTIC	MOLLIE BEATTIE	8,000,000.00	19,285,922.40	96-487	12-02-80
BECHAROF	BECHAROF	400,000.00	1,200,017.75	96-487	12-02-80
INNOKO	INNOKO	1,240,000.00	3,850,321.21	96-487	12-02-80
IZEMBEK	IZEMBEK	307,981.76	311,075.78	96-487	12-02-80
KENAI	KENAI	1,354,247.00	1,908,178.23	96-487	12-02-80
KOYUKUK	KOYUKUK	400,000.00	3,550,000.53	96-487	12-02-80
SELAWIK	SELAWIK	240,000.00	2,150,002.01	96-487	12-02-80
TOGIAK	TOGIAK	2,270,799.79	4,098,740.94	96-487	12-02-80
YUKON DELTA	ANDREAFSKY	1,300,000.00	19,166,094.48	96-487	12-02-80
	NUNIVAK	600,000.00		96-487	12-02-80
STATE TOTAL		18,689,348.55	58,985,600.12		
ARIZONA					
CABREZA PRIETA	CABEZA PRIETA	803,418.00	860,041.32	101-628	11-28-90
HAVASU	HAVASU	14,606.00	30,279.82	101-628	11-28-90
IMPERIAL	IMPERIAL REFUGE WILDERNESS	9,220.00	17,809.76	101-628	11-28-90
KOFA	KOFA	516,200.00	666,480.00	101-628	11-28-90
STATE TOTAL		1,343,444.00	1,574,610.90		
ARKANSAS					
BIG LAKE	BIG LAKE	2,143.80	11,036.10	94-557	10-19-76
STATE TOTAL		2,143.80	11,036.10		
CALIFORNIA					
FARALLON	FARALLON	141.00	211.00	93-550	12-26-74
HAVASU	HAVASU	3,195.00	7,235.34	103-433	10-31-94
IMPERIAL	IMPERIAL	5,836.00	7,958.19	103-433	10-31-94
STATE TOTAL		9,172.00	15,404.53		
COLORADO					
LEADVILLE *	MOUNT MASSIVE	2,560.00	3,065.88	96-560	12-22-80
STATE TOTAL		2,560.00	3,065.88		
FLORIDA					
CEDAR KEYS	CEDAR KEYS	379.00	891.15	92-364	08-07-72
CHASSAHOWITZKA	CHASSAHOWITZKA	23,578.93	30,842.91	94-557	10-19-76
GREAT WHITE HERON	FLORIDA KEYS	1,900.00	192,787.68	93-632	01-03-75
ISLAND BAY	ISLAND BAY	20.24	20.24	91-504	10-23-70
J.N. "DING" DARLING	J.N. "DING" DARLING	2,619.13	6,388.28	94-557	10-19-76
KEY WEST	FLORIDA KEYS	2,019.00	208,308.17	93-632	01-03-75
LAKE WOODRUFF	LAKE WOODRUFF	1,066.00	21,559.02	94-557	10-19-76
NATIONAL KEY DEER	FLORIDA KEYS(1)	2,278.00	8,952.31	93-632	01-03-75
PASSAGE KEY	PASSAGE KEY	36.37	63.87	91-504	10-23-70
PELICAN ISLAND	PELICAN ISLAND	5.50	5,375.93	91-504	10-23-70
ST. MARKS	ST. MARKS	17,350.00	67,623.07	93-632	01-03-75

STATE AND UNIT	WILDERNESS NAME	WILDERNESS ACRES	REFUGE ACRES	PUBLIC LAW NUMBER	PUBLIC LAW DATE
FLORIDA					
STATE TOTAL		51,252.17	542,812.58		
GEORGIA					
BLACKBEARD ISLAND	BLACKBEARD ISLAND	3,000.00	5,617.64	93-632	10-23-70
OKEFENOKEE	OKEFENOKEE	353,981.00	391,401.99	93-429	10-01-74
WOLF ISLAND	WOLF ISLAND	5,125.82	5,125.82	93-632	01-03-75
STATE TOTAL		362,106.82	402,145.45		
ILLINOIS					
CRAB ORCHARD	CRAB ORCHARD	4,050.00	43,888.52	94-557	10-19-76
STATE TOTAL		4,050.00	43,888.52		
LOUISIANA					
BRETON	BRETON	5,000.00	9,047.00	93-632	01-01-75
LACASSINE	LACASSINE	3,345.60	34,378.77	94-557	10-19-76
STATE TOTAL		8,345.60	43,425.77		
MAINE					
MOOSEHORN	BARING UNIT	4,680.00	27,680.45	93-632	01-03-75
	BIRCH ISLANDS UNIT	6.00		91-504	10-23-70
	EDMUNDS UNIT	2,706.00		91-504	10-23-70
STATE TOTAL		7,392.00	27,680.45		
MASSACHUSETTS					
MONOMOY	MONOMOY	2,420.00	2,701.85	91-504	10-23-70
STATE TOTAL		2,420.00	2,701.85		
MICHIGAN					
HURON	HURON ISLANDS	147.50	146.85	91-504	10-23-70
MICHIGAN ISLANDS	MICHIGAN ISLANDS	12.00	597.39	91-504	10-23-70
SENEY	SENEY	25,150.00	95,244.81	91-504	10-23-70
STATE TOTAL		25,309.50	95,989.05		
MINNESOTA					
AGASSIZ	AGASSIZ	4,000.00	61,500.93	94-557	10-19-76
TAMARAC	TAMARAC	2,180.00	35,191.38	94-557	10-19-76
STATE TOTAL		6,180.00	96,692.31		
MISSOURI					
MINGO	MINGO	7,730.00	21,745.86	94-557	10-19-76
STATE TOTAL		7,730.00	21,745.86		
MONTANA					
MEDICINE LAKE	MEDICINE LAKE	11,366.00	31,484.01	94-557	10-19-76
RED ROCK LAKES	RED ROCK LAKES	32,350.00	51,744.41	94-557	10-19-76
UL BEND	UL BEND	20,819.00	56,049.56	94-557	10-19-76
				98-140	10-31-83
STATE TOTAL		64,535.00	139,277.98		
NEBRASKA					
FORT NIOBRARA	FORT NIOBRARA	4,635.00	19,132.53	94-557	10-19-76
STATE TOTAL		4,635.00	19,132.53		
NEW JERSEY					
EDWIN B. FORSYTHE	BRIGANTINE	6,681.00	45,191.13	93-632	01-03-75
GREAT SWAMP	GREAT SWAMP	3,660.00	7,530.95	90-532	09-28-68
STATE TOTAL		10,341.00	52,722.08		
NEW MEXICO					
BITTER LAKE	SALT CREEK	9,621.00	24,608.64	91-504	10-23-70
BOSQUE DEL APACHE	CHUPADEA WILDERNESS AREA	5,289.00	57,191.10	93-632	01-03-75
	INDIAN WELL WILDERNESS AREA	5,139.00		93-632	01-03-75

STATE AND UNIT	WILDERNESS NAME	WILDERNESS ACRES	REFUGE ACRES	PUBLIC LAW	
				NUMBER	DATE
NEW MEXICO					
	LITTLE SAN PASCUAL WILDERNESS	19,859.00		93-632	01-03-75
STATE TOTAL		39,908.00	81,799.74		
NORTH CAROLINA					
SWANQUARTER	SWANQUARTER	8,784.93	16,411.09	94-557	10-19-76
STATE TOTAL		8,784.93	16,411.09		
NORTH DAKOTA					
CHASE LAKE	CHASE LAKE	4,155.00	4,449.47	93-632	01-03-75
LOSTWOOD	LOSTWOOD	5,577.00	26,903.99	96-632	01-03-75
STATE TOTAL		9,732.00	31,353.46		
OHIO					
WEST SISTER ISLAND	WEST SISTER ISLAND	77.00	80.13	93-632	01-03-75
STATE TOTAL		77.00	80.13		
OKLAHOMA					
WICHITA MOUNTAINS	CHARONS GARDEN UNIT	5,723.00	59,019.60	91-504	10-23-70
	NORTH MOUNTAIN UNIT	2,847.00		91-504	10-23-70
STATE TOTAL		8,570.00	59,019.60		
OREGON					
OREGON ISLANDS	OREGON ISLANDS	925.06	1,079.61	91-504	10-23-70
				95-450	10-11-78
				104-333	11-12-96
THREE ARCH ROCKS	THREE ARCH ROCKS	15.00	15.00	91-504	10-23-70
STATE TOTAL		925.06	1,094.61		
SOUTH CAROLINA					
CAPE ROMAIN	CAPE ROMAIN	29,000.00	65,224.94	93-632	01-03-75
STATE TOTAL		29,000.00	65,224.94		
WASHINGTON					
COPALIS	WASHINGTON ISLANDS	60.80	60.80	91-504	10-23-70
FLATTERY ROCKS	WASHINGTON ISLANDS	125.00	125.00	91-504	10-23-70
QUILLAYUTE NEEDLES	WASHINGTON ISLANDS	300.20	300.20	91-504	10-23-70
SAN JUAN ISLANDS	SAN JUAN ISLANDS	353.00	448.53	94-557	10-19-76
STATE TOTAL		839.00	934.53		
WISCONSIN					
GRAVEL ISLAND	WISCONSIN ISLANDS	27.00	27.00	91-504	10-23-70
GREEN BAY	WISCONSIN ISLANDS	2.00	2.00	91-504	10-23-70
STATE TOTAL		29.00	29.00		
GRAND TOTAL		20,698,845.43	62,290,453.29		

* Located on the Leadville National Fish Hatchery

TABLE 9 - MIGRATORY WATERFOWL REFUGES ON FEDERAL WATER RESOURCE PROJECTS

UNITS ALSO INCLUDED IN TABLE 3

STATE AND UNIT	ACRES UNDER PRIMARY CONTROL OF				TOTAL ACRES
	CORPS OF ENGINEERS	BUREAU OF RECLAMATION	TENNESSEE VALLEY AUTHORITY	FISH AND WILDLIFE SERVICE	
ALABAMA					
CHOCTAW	4,218.00	0.00	0.00	0.00	4,218.00
EUFAULA	7,929.00	0.00	0.00	24.19	7,953.19
WHEELER	0.00	0.00	25,674.62	8,756.04	34,430.66
STATE TOTAL	12,147.00	0.00	25,674.62	8,780.23	46,601.85
ARIZONA					
BILL WILLIAMS	0.00	1,699.07	0.00	4,355.69	6,054.76
CIBOLA	0.00	623.38	0.00	7,982.66	8,606.04
HAVASU	0.00	20,235.28	0.00	10,044.54	30,279.82
IMPERIAL	0.00	17,166.14	0.00	643.62	17,809.76
STATE TOTAL	0.00	39,723.87	0.00	23,026.51	62,750.38
ARKANSAS					
WHITE RIVER	45.80	0.00	0.00	158,368.92	158,414.72
STATE TOTAL	45.80	0.00	0.00	158,368.92	158,414.72
CALIFORNIA					
CLEAR LAKE	0.00	33,440.00	0.00	15,020.07	46,460.07
HAVASU	0.00	7,225.34	0.00	10.00	7,235.34
IMPERIAL	0.00	7,958.19	0.00	0.00	7,958.19
SONNY BONO SALTON SEA	0.00	23,424.58	0.00	14,234.29	37,658.87
STATE TOTAL	0.00	72,048.11	0.00	27,264.36	99,312.47
GEORGIA					
EUFAULA	3,231.00	0.00	0.00	0.00	3,231.00
STATE TOTAL	3,231.00	0.00	0.00	0.00	3,231.00
IDAHO					
DEER FLAT	0.00	9,993.28	0.00	1,272.11	11,265.39
MINIDOKA	0.00	17,835.19	0.00	2,866.42	20,701.61
STATE TOTAL	0.00	27,828.47	0.00	4,138.53	31,967.00
ILLINOIS					
GREAT RIVER	5,490.81	0.00	0.00	1,619.82	7,110.63
PORT LOUISA	1,466.00	0.00	0.00	4.89	1,470.89
TWO RIVERS	7,017.00	0.00	0.00	1,016.20	8,033.20
UPPER MISSISSIPPI RIVER	20,120.00	0.00	0.00	3,312.73	23,432.73
STATE TOTAL	34,093.81	0.00	0.00	5,953.64	40,047.45
IOWA					
PORT LOUISA	10,423.94	0.00	0.00	12,199.43	22,623.37
UPPER MISSISSIPPI RIVER	30,315.00	0.00	0.00	20,724.21	51,039.21
STATE TOTAL	40,738.94	0.00	0.00	32,923.64	73,662.58
KANSAS					
FLINT HILLS	18,463.21	0.00	0.00	.15	18,463.36
KIRWIN	0.00	10,778.00	0.00	0.00	10,778.00
STATE TOTAL	18,463.21	10,778.00	0.00	.15	29,241.36
MINNESOTA					
BIG STONE	254.20	0.00	0.00	11,265.93	11,520.13
UPPER MISSISSIPPI RIVER	15,420.77	0.00	0.00	18,248.03	33,668.80
STATE TOTAL	15,674.97	0.00	0.00	29,513.96	45,188.93
MISSISSIPPI					
PANTHER SWAMP	7,070.45	0.00	0.00	28,201.40	35,271.85
STATE TOTAL	7,070.45	0.00	0.00	28,201.40	35,271.85
MISSOURI					
TWO RIVERS	232.00	0.00	0.00	0.00	232.00
STATE TOTAL	232.00	0.00	0.00	0.00	232.00
MONTANA					
CHARLES M. RUSSELL	528,300.14	0.00	0.00	384,048.18	912,348.32

STATE AND UNIT	ACRES UNDER PRIMARY CONTROL OF				TOTAL ACRES
	CORPS OF ENGINEERS	BUREAU OF RECLAMATION	TENNESSEE VALLEY AUTHORITY	FISH AND WILDLIFE SERVICE	
MONTANA					
UL BEND	14,823.36	0.00	0.00	41,226.20	56,049.56
STATE TOTAL	543,123.50	0.00	0.00	425,274.38	968,397.83
NEBRASKA					
NORTH PLATTE	0.00	2,684.81	0.00	788.42	3,473.23
STATE TOTAL	0.00	2,684.81	0.00	788.42	3,473.23
NEVADA					
FALLON	0.00	17,901.94	0.00	0.00	17,901.94
STATE TOTAL	0.00	17,901.94	0.00	0.00	17,901.94
NEW MEXICO					
MAXWELL	0.00	438.52	0.00	3,260.07	3,698.59
STATE TOTAL	0.00	438.52	0.00	3,260.07	3,698.59
NORTH DAKOTA					
AUDUBON	14,739.19	0.00	0.00	0.00	14,739.19
STATE TOTAL	14,739.19	0.00	0.00	0.00	14,739.19
OKLAHOMA					
OPTIMA	4,332.81	0.00	0.00	0.00	4,332.81
SALT PLAINS	11,565.28	0.00	0.00	20,491.84	32,057.12
SEQUOYAH	20,800.00	0.00	0.00	0.00	20,800.00
TISHOMINGO	16,464.18	0.00	0.00	0.00	16,464.18
WASHITA	0.00	8,061.81	0.00	13.56	8,075.37
STATE TOTAL	53,162.27	8,061.81	0.00	20,505.40	81,729.48
OREGON					
COLD SPRINGS	0.00	2,679.95	0.00	436.88	3,116.83
MCKAY CREEK	0.00	1,813.00	0.00	23.50	1,836.50
UMATILLA	7,430.37	0.00	0.00	1,477.00	8,907.37
STATE TOTAL	7,430.37	4,492.95	0.00	1,937.38	13,860.70
SOUTH CAROLINA					
TYBEE	100.00	0.00	0.00	0.00	100.00
STATE TOTAL	100.00	0.00	0.00	0.00	100.00
TENNESSEE					
CROSS CREEKS	2,442.00	0.00	0.00	6,419.49	8,861.49
TENNESSEE	0.00	0.00	50,830.30	529.16	51,359.46
STATE TOTAL	2,442.00	0.00	50,830.30	6,948.65	60,220.95
TEXAS					
HAGERMAN	11,319.84	0.00	0.00	0.00	11,319.84
STATE TOTAL	11,319.84	0.00	0.00	0.00	11,319.84
WASHINGTON					
COLUMBIA	0.00	2,662.00	0.00	26,934.27	29,596.27
MCNARY	11,895.00	0.00	0.00	3,630.70	15,525.70
UMATILLA	13,209.50	0.00	0.00	1,666.33	14,875.83
STATE TOTAL	25,104.50	2,662.00	0.00	32,231.30	59,997.80
WISCONSIN					
UPPER MISSISSIPPI	40,341.00	0.00	0.00	48,994.54	89,335.54
STATE TOTAL	40,341.00	0.00	0.00	48,994.54	88,335.54
WYOMING					
PATHFINDER	0.00	14,512.06	0.00	2,294.84	16,806.90
STATE TOTAL	0.00	14,512.06	0.00	2,294.84	16,806.90
GRAND TOTAL	829,459.85	201,132.54	76,504.92	860,406.32	1,967,503.63

Notes

In addition to the changes noted in the accomplishments on page 6 and those noted below, the figures in our tables may show some changes from previous annual reports. For example, decreases in acreage figures may reflect expired leases, real property disposals made in land exchanges, or property transfers. An increase or decrease may be noted after new property surveys are completed or when additional information is entered into the database after the data has been transmitted from the regions for publication. Other changes result from corrections that are made when errors are found in the historical data previously entered into the database systems or when information was not previously entered into the database (e.g., see Table 3, Don Edwards San Francisco Bay NWR in California where the total acreage is corrected by deleting double entries and Palmyra Atoll NWR in Palmyra Atoll where the calculation of the submerged lands within the 12-mile limit changed).

Table 2A: Negative acreage will appear in Table 2A when we dispose of or transfer more acres than we acquire in that state during the fiscal year. For example, two leases totaling 3,930 acres expired on Alligator River NWR in North Carolina.

Table 3: Four additional refuges were established: Detroit River International Wildlife Refuge in Michigan, Bayou Teche National Wildlife Refuge and Red River National Wildlife Refuge in Louisiana, and Cahaba River National Wildlife Refuge in Alabama. Public Law 107-91 includes the existing 327-acre Wyandotte NWR in the boundary of the Detroit River International Wildlife Refuge. The Wyandotte Refuge will no longer appear in this report but the acreage is included in the Detroit River IWR (also see Accomplishments section of this report).

In addition to establishing four new refuges, the Service expanded the existing Northern Tallgrass Prairie National Wildlife Refuge in Minnesota into the State of Iowa. Although the new acreage will appear under Iowa, it is not counted as a new refuge.

Tables 3 and 4: The report summarizes Farm Service Agency (formerly Farmers Home Administration), Department of Agriculture, units in Table 3 by state and in Table 4 by state and county. These entries, identified as "FSA Interest" consist of lands or interests in lands acquired from the Farm Service Agency that are not located within existing project boundaries. We include FSA units in state and county acreage totals, but do not count them as separate units.

Table 4: The Waterfowl Production Areas are units of the National Wildlife Refuge System established under the Migratory Bird Conservation Act. For purposes of this report, the acreage of the WPAs are rolled up by county in each state and the total number of NWRS Waterfowl Production Area units are shown as the total number of approved counties with WPA acres.

A new Minnesota Waterfowl Production Area County, Waseca, is added to Table 4 under the Minnesota Valley Wetland Management District.

Table 6: We conveyed an excess bunkhouse building in the village of Kaktovik to the local community. The bunkhouse is on land owned by the village.

Table 7: The Ouray hatchery in Utah is counted as a National Fish Hatchery but it is located on the Ouray National Wildlife Refuge and the acreage is included in Table 3 rather than Table 7.

The Hagerman National Fish Hatchery in Idaho is managed by the Service, but the remainder of the land is managed by the State and appears in Table 5 as the Hagerman Coordination Area. In Fiscal Year 1996 the majority of real property at the 130-acre New London National Fish Hatchery (NFH) was transferred to the State of Minnesota to be used by the State for fishery resources management in accordance with Public Law 104-25. The remaining 2.5 acres were transferred in Fiscal Year 2002 and no longer appear in this report (not previously counted as a national fish hatchery). Also, a 32.07-acre lease from the Mescalero Tribe was terminated, and the Mescalero NFH in New Mexico will no longer appear in this report.

Table 8: An additional 4,247 acres were acquired within the Wilderness area of the Kenai National Wildlife Refuge in Alaska.

www.ingramcontent.com/pod-product-compliance
Lightning Source LLC
Chambersburg PA
CBHW052014280526
45793CB00005B/978